THE

MW00875522

OF
ORGANIZATION

Take Back Your House
One Phase at a Time

LISA WOODRUFF

Copyright © 2016 Lisa Woodruff

All rights reserved. No part of this publication may be reproduced, distributed, or transmitted in any form or by any means, including photocopying, recording, or other electronic or mechanical methods, without the prior written permission of the publisher, except in the case of brief quotations embodied in reviews and certain other non-commercial uses permitted by copyright law.

ISBN 10: 1537105477
ISBN-13: 978-1537105475

This book is dedicated to all the women who have allowed me into their organizational journeys. I have enjoyed every step.

To my mother for letting me practice my organizing and telling me I can do anything I set my mind to.

To my children Joey and Abby.
Being your mom is my greatest blessing.

And to my husband Greg.
Thanks for all your encouragement and support as I have chased my dreams.

TABLE OF CONTENTS

INTRODUCTION

A Guide to This Book

As a professional organizer and productivity expert, I have noticed that my clients go through four distinct phases of life when it comes to organization. Whether or not a woman chooses to marry or start a family, she will go through each of these phases at roughly the same times in her life. There really is no denying that as the decades go by, women's organizational needs and the demands on their time will change.

Most organizational books on the market profess to have a one-size-fits-all solution to home organization. This one does not.

I hate to break it to you, but as you transition from one phase of life to the next, you will need to reevaluate and change up your organizational systems. Knowing what phase of life you are in will help you to learn the skills you need to get organized.

So what phase of life are you in?

Seven to Twenty-One: Childhood and Adolescence

The first phase of organization is from the age of seven to around twenty-one. It is during this phase of life that you learn to take care of your bedroom, clothing, toys, and personal possessions.

There are four basic steps to organizing your room, steps that you should do every single week.

Twenty-One to Forty: Accumulation

After you graduate from college and move out into the big wide world, you start to develop your own identity and life.

You acquire houses, spouses, children, careers, and all of the pieces and parts that go along with those responsibilities.

During these years, organization is all about creating new systems for all the new things that are coming into your life. And while some decluttering and purging does happen, more often you're looking for solutions to store items you're not currently using, in case they are needed for additional children or a bigger house.

Forty to Fifty-Five: Survival

Somewhere around the age of forty a switch flips in your mind, and you suddenly have a different perspective than you did in your twenties and thirties.

The woman in her forties or early fifties has a great sense of perspective and a wealth of knowledge. What she does not have is time. Everyone needs her, and she wants to help everyone who is close to her.

She is never at home. Her days are spent ferrying children here and there and providing for her household. The days spent at home with young children are long gone, and household projects pile up quickly.

The organizational challenge for the woman in this phase of life is to create systems and order in her home so that she has as much time as possible available to help and serve others.

Fifty-Five and Up: Downsizing and Legacy

In this phase of life, a woman is focused on downsizing the house she is currently in, determining what items she wants to save and preserve for future generations, and deciding what her legacy will be.

It is in these years that she is of most service to the community. She can offer wisdom to future generations, and she has realized that life is shorter than she ever expected it to be.

Women in this phase of life often focus on organizing their photos and memorabilia, along with their children's prized possessions that were left in their attics, basements, and bedrooms. Throughout their lifetimes, the pendulum has swung from a focus on material accumulation to a desire to leave a legacy for a lighter, more agile generation—one which tends to be averse to accumulating "stuff," no matter how nice it is.

Is This Book for You?

Organization is more than just fifteen-minute daily tasks and fun ways to use cute containers. This book is designed for women who are ready to take back control of their homes.

Understanding the four organizational phases of life will help you to identify and solve the organizational dilemmas you face. It will also give you the perspective to see the organizational phases your parents and children are currently in, so you can help in their organizing efforts as well.

How This Book Works

Join with me as I take you on the journey of home organization through all four phases of life. For each of the first three phases, I will share with you my own journey, some concrete action steps to get you started, and ideas for saving memories and mementos from that time of life.

I have not entered the fourth phase yet, but my company, Organize 365, has helped hundreds of women downsize their homes and preserve their legacies for future generations. In this chapter, I will share with you how different generations look at "stuff" and how to decide what to part with.

The final chapter of the book covers home organization plans and maintenance. You'll also find information on my whole-house challenge options, which will guide you through the process of getting your whole house organized, one day at a time.

How Do I Know This Will Work?

I was a "born organized" person. And for years I served my family, friends, and clients with my talents, thinking I was just born this way.

And then a funny thing happened . . .

I organized a seven-year-old's bedroom with her and her bedroom was still organized six months later.

And I ran out of clients! Even my clients with ADHD didn't need my services anymore, because their homes didn't get UN-organized. The icing on the cake was when a few of my clients started their own professional organization businesses.

Once I saw that my clients were maintaining their organization consistently, I knew that the skill of being organized was teachable.

The Cincinnati Organize 365 team has been able to organize hundreds of houses, and thousands more women have followed my blog and podcasts to achieve order in their homes. Understanding the organizational struggles that are inherent in your phase of life is a game changer.

As you follow along on my organizational journey, you will see the strategies I employed to get organized—and how I navigated the inevitable rough transitions from one phase of life to the next.

Let's start at the beginning.

PUZZLES

The buzzer sounded and we sprang into action. My grandma flipped the box. I glanced quickly at the picture and then, as quick as I could, flipped and sorted. Edge pieces toward the bottom of the table, the rest sorted by color. Within twenty minutes, we were snapping pieces together.

My love affair with jigsaw puzzles started when I was very young. My seasonal asthma was so severe, I was hospitalized four times in my second year of life. After multiple daily medications and many doctor's appointments—not to mention the donation of all my stuffed animals—my asthma settled into a semi-annual, week-long period of bedridden sickness. The illness was punctuated by a middle-of-the-night drive to the hospital for a shot of epinephrine.

It was during one of these week-long illnesses that my grandmother brought me a puzzle to work on in bed. Doing a puzzle was about the only thing I could do besides read a book when it hurt just to breathe.

Later, when I was older and my asthma was better under control, I would sometimes spend the night at Grandma's. She always had a puzzle going. Her house was so quiet. In the evening, when the grandfather clock's chimes tolled nine, I would grow quiet, too. My normal chattiness vanished as I hoped that I could stay up later and continue to "work the puzzle" with Grandma. As the clock chimed, I'd hold my breath.

Yes! Another fifteen minutes. I'd work feverishly to see how much more I could accomplish before the next clock chime.

Now here I was, a thirteen-year-old girl in the gym at Ohio University, competing with hundreds of other two-woman teams to see who could complete their puzzle the fastest. Each team had an eight-foot table covered in white paper, on which lay a brand-new, never-seen-before, thousand-piece Springbok puzzle.

I have a photographic memory, as I imagine many other jigsaw puzzle lovers do. Having a brand new puzzle leveled the playing field. The winning team completed their puzzle in just under two hours. Grandma and I were closer to four.

I spent much of my childhood with the women in my mother's and grandmother's generations. This trip was no exception. I was by far the youngest in attendance.

We met so many nice ladies on our trip. One of them had done some unofficial research and found that all jigsaw puzzle lovers also loved to read, but not all readers loved to do jigsaw puzzles. I would guess that many professional organizers also love jigsaw puzzles.

Give me a rainy day, a new jigsaw puzzle, a great movie, a bubbly fountain Coke, and I am in heaven. I love the challenge of sorting and fitting all those random pieces into a beautiful picture. It wasn't until I was in my forties that I realized I could be paid to do real-life jigsaw puzzles.

I had just launched my professional organization business and was helping a mother organize her master closet, garage, and kitchen. We planned to complete one space per day.

In my thirties, I had cleaned houses, so I knew how nice it was to take a house from dirty to clean in a matter of hours. It wasn't like my clients couldn't clean their homes. They just didn't have the time or desire to do so.

In my opinion, "organizing" was just deeper cleaning in an area the client couldn't get under control. I really thought it was a lack of time and ideas problem. Because organizing came so easily to me, I hadn't really thought about the fact that what I did was anything special.

At the end of the first day, my client broke down in tears. I was worried she was upset with me. Oh, no! Had I pushed her too far? The donations were still piled in my car; we could bring them back into the house.

"I could actually go back to work," she said. "I never thought I would ever be able to leave the house again, and now I think I could go back to work."

All because I organized a closet? I still hadn't grasped the toll disorganization could take on a family—and especially on its women.

The next day, we set out to tackle the garage. I surveyed the room and then walked to a corner and started pairing like items together, making piles for the client to sort. A few hours later, we were side by side when she held up a pink crock and said, "Where is the other crock?"

Without looking up I said, "Behind me to the left in the far corner."

"What?!" she said. "It IS there!"

I looked up and saw her dumbfounded, holding two pink crocks. Huh. You mean everyone doesn't take a picture of the room with their mind and sort the pieces into a finished room?

By the end of the week, my client's master closet was done. Her car was in the garage for the first time since she bought the house. When we organized the kitchen, we found a tax rebate check that could not be reissued. By finding that rebate check (which had fallen out of a kitchen drawer and behind the cabinet), she actually MADE money by having me come organize. A few months later, she was employed and coming out the far side of a long depression.

I always knew my love of jigsaw puzzles was not shared by all, but what I realized that week was that my talent for being able to envision a completed picture from a bunch of mixed-up pieces was more useful than I'd realized. I had unknowingly honed a skill that could dramatically change a woman's life in a matter of days.

Over the next few years, I worked feverishly to organize and streamline the houses of my clients, as well as my own home. I had an overabundance of adrenaline and ideas. At the end of a long day, I'd be physically exhausted, but my mind would be working in overdrive, looking for more items to purge, more systems to implement, and more spaces to declutter.

I was afraid our house would be empty because I continued to get rid of items from our home when I returned from sessions with clients.

The more houses I organized, the more I realized organization was a skill. Once my clients learned the skill, they no longer needed me. But even more surprising, they began organizing their friends' homes, too. My mission became teaching others the skill of home organization and the confidence to take back their homes.

As you may imagine, I have consumed most of the books available on the topics of home organization and productivity. You can find my most up-to-date home organization tips and strategies at www.organize365.com.

THE FOUR PHASES OF LIFE

This book is all about the organizational journey a woman takes from age seven to eighty-seven. In each of the four stages of life, I will share with you my personal organization journey, as well as stories from my clients. As you discover the picture of how each stage of life looks when organized, you will be able to jump in and put the pieces of your daily puzzle in place.

First, let's take a deeper look at all four phases of life.

Seven to Twenty-One: Childhood and Adolescence

The first phase of organization is from the age of seven to around twenty-one. How you organized your bedroom as a child and the skills you learned during that time really do translate to how you organize your house.

I teach children to view their bedroom like it is their own mini-apartment.

I am sure this is not breaking news for you, but understanding, implementing, and learning these skills at a young age will set you up for success in each subsequent phase of life.

The prevailing myth is that children are either born organized or they aren't. That just isn't true. Organization is a skill that can be learned by anyone in any phase of life.

The earlier the better.

Twenty-one to Forty: Accumulation

When puppies and babies come into the world, they can't organize themselves, that's for sure. Our little puppy has a toy bin in the family room. After I clean up all the toys, he will go over and get them out when he's bored.

When you have a baby, every two to three months, the baby needs a whole new wardrobe, sometimes a whole new diet, and of course, new toys. Children start with bouncy seats, car seats, and strollers, then quickly move into exersaucers, swings, and high chairs. Once they're mobile, they'll get a train table, and a few years later, a Lego table. If you're in this stage of life, you're likely thinking, "Oh, I have all that and more."

As your child goes from zero to three months, three to six months, six to nine months, and finally to one year old, they will probably have enough stuff to fill a whole condo. But you're not going to get rid of the exersaucer, the boppy, and the swing, even though they're done with them, because you're in the accumulation phase of life and you're going to have more kids. You may not have decided how many kids that's going to be yet. And sometimes at forty, surprise, you have one more.

Having lived through this phase in its entirety, one of the clutter tips I employed was to sell things at garage sales and buy them again later.

Your energy level in the accumulation stage is a huge bonus. I know you're sleep deprived and you're thinking, "You've got to be kidding me. I do not have energy." Let me just tell you, you have more energy now than you will ever have again.

When I wanted to redo a kids' room when I was in my twenties, it was done before the end of the day. My husband would come home from work and say, "Didn't that room use to be blue and now it's pink?" I'd say, "Yeah, it did."

Because I got up at seven that morning, put the little kids in their strollers, and pushed them off to the hardware store to get the paint. I'd come home, put them in the exersaucer, and I would paint. I had so much energy and so many ideas and so much drive that I could just get so much done.

Women who work outside the home in this phase of life are no exception. They too can accomplish big projects in just a few short days.

Forty to Fifty-Five: Survival

The woman in her forties to early fifties usually has children in middle school, high school, and college. Often, it is during this time that she will return to the workforce either part-time, full-time, or from home.

According to the US Department of Labor, in the United States, 70 percent of women with children under the age of eighteen are employed.[1] They're preparing for the upcoming college tuition bills, and they want to continue to build their nest egg for retirement so that they can, hopefully, get back to doing something with this husband that they love.

Unfortunately, this is also usually the time of life when a woman needs to start caring for her parents or taking care of a friend who has become gravely ill. She may go through a divorce. The needs of both her children and her parents on her time ushers her into the sandwich generation.

When you join the sandwich generation, you really are just surviving day to day. Not that you're not enjoying your life. I would say my friends in their forties are enjoying life more than they did in their twenties and thirties, but it is a survival game.

---

[1] Bureau of Labor Statistics, Current Population Survey (CPS), https://www.dol.gov/wb/stats/stats_data.htm.

Even if a woman had the little bonus baby, she's not the same parent of that baby as she was of the baby that she had in her twenties. She parents differently. The new baby is raised on the soccer fields and is always in the car and on the go.

If you didn't have children in your twenties and you have your first children in your late thirties, it's likely that you also won't raise your children as twenty-year-old parents do. You'll probably do it more like a forty or fifty-year-old mother would.

It is not unusual for me to talk to somebody in this phase of life and say, "Okay, tell me where you drive your kids." And then I say, "Do you realize you have a part-time (or a full-time) driving job?" That's when it hits them like a ton of bricks. "No wonder I can't get anything done at home. I'm working forty hours a week and I'm driving forty hours a week. It makes sense that there is no time for me to get the laundry done anymore because I'm just never physically at home to do the laundry."

Often, this is also the time of life where women who got divorced in their late thirties return to the work force as a single parent.

During this decade and a half, some kind of major tragedy will likely happen to you—probably multiple major tragedies—and you'll be in charge of them. It's also the time of life where your parents will likely get sick or pass away.

So on top of the job and driving the kids everywhere, you're also in charge of an older family member. This is why it's called the sandwich generation. You're smooched and wringed and pressed down, and there is just no time to breathe.

Even though you're getting pressed down and you have a ridiculous amount of responsibility, you're able to handle it better. I don't know how to explain it. You have a better perspective now, and you don't worry about things.

When I turned forty it was like something just clicked in my brain. I remember my friend told me this would happen. You have your fortieth birthday and think, "Oh my gosh, I'm going to be forty. I'm a dinosaur, I should just die now."

And then a couple days later, you're thinking, "You know what? I don't care what anybody thinks anymore. I really don't care. I don't care that you don't want my kids in this after-school program, I'm putting them there anyway. I don't care that you don't like that I don't vaccinate my kids. I'll just decide if I do or don't vaccinate my kids."

That issue in your twenties or thirties, whether or not you're going to vaccinate your children, would have caused you to write letters to congressmen and put it all over Facebook. You would have been up in arms that everybody has to vaccinate or not vaccinate their kids.

By the time you're in your forties, you think, "That's great. You do whatever you want, I'm going to do whatever I want. I'm comfortable with my decision, you be comfortable with your decision."

It was so liberating to me in my forties to finally feel like I knew what the heck I was doing. I'm comfortable in the woman I am for the children that I have, for the spouse that I have, and for the responsibilities that I have. I'm going to work at home, drive thirty hours a week, put my kids in a really expensive elementary school, and not put them in a traditional four-year college. I'm fine with that. I'm over trying to get the whole world to realize that not every kid is going to go to college. I know what's good for my kids and my family.

That happens in your forties.

Then sometime between your fifties and sixties (I am forty-four, so I can't really say exactly when it happens, but I see it with my clients), you move into this next phase that I call the downsizing and legacy phase.

Fifty-Five and Up: Downsizing and Legacy

A woman in this phase of life is actively engaged in her children's lives. She's able to do with her grandchildren the things that she did not have time to do when she was in the survival phase of life.

When my father passed away, my sister and I had to handle the estate, which meant cleaning out and selling the family home. Once you bury a parent and you have to get your family home ready for sale, you start looking at your own house in a totally different light. At some point along the way, you realize that all of the stuff in that house doesn't go with you, and it will end up sitting there for whoever is left to take care of it.

Then you start to say to yourself, "I don't think that I want anybody else to have to clean this stuff out of my house." You start to realize you keep things you don't need in case you need them someday. Crazy stuff.

Here's an example: You have a party and you have an extra ten cups that are pink, and you keep those because the next time you have a party, you don't want to have to buy those expensive pink cups again. But let me just give you a clue. The next time you have a party, even if you only invite ten people, you're still going to buy more pink cups because you're afraid you're not going to have enough, and then there will be forty pink cups in your basement. Because this is just how we are.

Here's another example. I was going to can fruits and vegetables about a decade ago. So, of course, I have mason jars in my basement. Finally, last year I thought, "Okay, I'm not going to even make a craft out of them, and I for sure am not going to be canning." I donated the mason jars.

When you don't clean out those projects that are never going to happen in your house, here is what happens. Eventually, you pass away. Every single thing in your house takes on an exponential importance because you bought it and you touched it.

When you're in grief and you're trying to make decisions about how to get rid of everything that's in the home that you lived in for thirty-five years, it is so hard to have perspective and say, "Photographs, we save. Those are meaningful. Mason jars that you can buy for ten dollars at the store, we let go."

It's really, really hard to make that decision because you have grief brain. I see it in my clients all the time. In my observation, it takes five years to get through it. On average, pretty much to the day, it's five years. There is no way to speed it up, and you're not going to keep the family home for five years while you decide if you're going to keep mason jars or not.

Having gone through that experience of helping someone clean out their family home, you think, "Why am I keeping five mattresses in my attic? Why do I need to have four sets of dishes?" And you start to purge things.

You also start to think about your legacy in this stage of life. This is often when people will hire me to make photo albums.

Now that you've identified which phase of life you are in, let's talk about the three stages of actually getting organized.

THE THREE STAGES OF ORGANIZATION

Just like there are four distinct phases of life I see a woman go through, there are three distinct stages of organization that any one woman can land in.

Stage 1: Complete Overwhelm

If you are in this stage of organization, you probably don't need me to expound any further.

- You don't know where to begin.
- It seems pointless to even start.
- The project is going to take so long that you can't imagine when it will be completed.
- You listen to a podcast, read a blog post, or watch a TV episode about getting organized and are super excited until you turn around and look at your own organizational challenge. Suddenly you are frozen in place.

In this stage of organization, it is helpful to only think about two things:

1. What is trash?
2. What do you no longer want and love? What you are free to donate?

Honestly, when you are in an overwhelmed state, you can go through a whole house organization challenge just throwing away trash and stuffing bags full of items to donate.

<u>Because I hate to break it to you</u>, but you cannot organize an overwhelming amount of clutter. Your only choice is to get rid of some things in order to get a more organized, calm, and peaceful living space.

Step 1 — Get black trash bags. Take a black trash bag and go into whatever room you're going to declutter. Your only job is to fill that black trash bag with trash.

Step 2 — Once you have all the trash gone, then you're going to go back into the same room and donate every single thing that you don't love or need. Then take that second black trash bag straight out to the car to be donated.

You will be amazed at what progress you will make by just starting to identify what is trash and what you no longer need in your house and getting it out.

Most people are able to eliminate 50 percent of what's in a room. If you are in the overwhelmed stage, that means every drawer is a junk drawer, every flat surface has piles of stuff on it. Your clean laundry is either on your bed or your couch, but it's not put away.

I know how you live. This is not judgment, this is just reality. You are overwhelmed, and when you are overwhelmed, you have to reduce the amount you're looking at. We cannot talk about organizing your sock drawer if all of your socks are in the laundry room, right?

And we can't talk about organizing your library if you have books in every single room of your house like I did. The first step is to get rid of as much as we can that we know we don't need.

And that is exactly what I did when I was so overwhelmed with the disorganization in my own house. The first time, I did my own whole house challenge. I went into every single space and I just got rid of as much as I physically could and ended up with 50 percent of our house left.

When I was done, I realized that it wasn't organized, but I was ready to get organized. I'm telling you this as a professional organizer. It took me forty days just to get rid of the stuff that I didn't need. And I barely made that timetable because it is so mentally exhausting getting rid of stuff you don't need. It really is hard.

Stage 2: Systems and Organization

In the second stage of organization, there are still things that need to be donated (and, occasionally, trash) in the areas that you go to organize. However, at this point you can actually see places that need to be organized, and you're not completely overwhelmed as soon as you walk into the space.

While the task may still be daunting, if you start in one corner of the room, you can work your way around to the other corner in a matter of hours, days, or at least within one week.

In Stage 2, the key is to find one area inside the room that you're going to tackle first. Once you have succeeded, move on to the next area. Tackling all the drawers in your kitchen is much more doable than saying you're going to "organize the entire kitchen."

Keep your challenges manageable. Work within the amount of time you have available to you. Keep focusing on the areas that you have already organized. Don't look at how much is left to be done.

The second time I went through a whole house organizing challenge, I was able to eliminate another 25 percent of what I had saved.

Stage 2 is still eliminating. For the first fifteen minutes you're going to say, "Okay, what in here don't I need, love, and want?" After that, you're going to be creating systems and actually organizing.

Let's take the kitchen, for example. The first time through, you're just getting rid of everything you don't use, like the waffle maker you got eighteen years ago that's still in the box and the broken blender. In Stage 2, you're going to go through every drawer and cabinet making more refined choices.

"Okay, we don't need eighteen spatulas, we only need three. We only have one pizza cutter, but we actually need two, so I'm going to buy one." You can make those kinds of decisions. You're going to purge, and then the organizing starts.

But you're also going to add, and you're going to say, "I'm going to get some baskets and organize these drawers." Or, "I'm going to redo the pantry today. I'm going to pull everything out and redo the shelves, and then I'm going to put everything back in."

Stage 3: Refining Your Systems and Maintaining

I'm going to be honest here, I did not get to this level of organization until the third time that I organized my whole house.

Organization is not a destination, it is a journey. We are never going to be "completely organized."

But each time that you do even one thing to maintain or create more organization in your life, you move closer to living a more organized everyday life.

In this stage of organization, you may choose to invest in some cute magazine-type organization products that are just pure fun. Or decorative.

It is also in this stage of organization that you are able to organize the entire kitchen in a matter of hours. The storage room that used to take you a week to organize will now be able to be organized in one day.

While the need to maintain your home and continue to organize it does not go away, the amount of time, effort, and resources necessary to do so diminishes greatly.

In the third stage, there will be very little to donate. You will usually be able to declutter anything that needs to be decluttered in about fifteen minutes per space. Then you will be able to go through and freshen up the organization in about an hour per space.

That's when you'll be able to say, "Okay, I put this organizational system in place last year. I kind of like it, but I don't love it, so I'm going to tweak it." Or, "This year, I'm going to invest in those spinning spice rack things Lisa talked about. I've loved those for years and I think they're a great solution for me."

As you read through the following chapters, you will begin to see how you learned—or did not learn—the organizational lessons of each phase of life. Let's head back to childhood.

Phase One

CHILDHOOD AND ADOLESCENCE

My Childhood
Organizational Journey

ven though I was "born organized," as I transitioned into each new phase of my life, I reached a crisis point and had to change my organization to fit my phase of life. As you read my story, think about your children (if you have them) and see if you also have a "born organized" child in your midst.

Organizing My Bedroom

The first time I really remember being organized, or where I can pinpoint starting my organization journey, was when I would get punished and sent to my bedroom for time-out. Now that I work from home and have a home-based business, I understand why this was my mom's discipline method of choice. When you send your children to their room for a period of time, you're able to get more business done. I think that's what my mom was doing.

Once we were in our bedrooms, my sister Emily and I would instantly become best friends again, which would break up whatever fight we were having. Now, my sister is a very social person, so she was chomping at the bit to get out of her room, back to where the people were. But I was like, "Okay, while I'm in here for X amount of time, what can I do to be productive?" I was always trying to be productive, so I would spend that time organizing my room.

When I got older, I would also rearrange the furniture in my room, and my organization became more detailed. If I was going to organize the closet, I figured I might as well take everything out of the closet first. Once everything was out of the closet, I would add an organizational element or move a shelf. I would analyze every single piece of clothing and toy as I put it back into the closet.

As soon as the timer went off and my sister and I were done with time-out, my sister would be out of her room and into mine. I wouldn't be done organizing yet, because I loved what I was doing. By this point, I would have moved from the closet into the bedroom itself, or perhaps under the bed. I was organizing everything!

While I was organizing, I would make a pile of stuff that I didn't want anymore. I would ask Emily, "Do you want any of this stuff?" And she would usually take almost all of it to her room. A couple of years later, she told me the reason why she was disorganized was because I was constantly giving her my castoffs and she was saving them all.

Organizing Other Family Spaces

I got bored organizing my room and wanted to organize other spaces in our house, but I wasn't bold enough to organize the kitchen or family room. And honestly, our house was not disorganized. Which really frustrated me sometimes because I was looking for a real-life puzzle to do!

My father always had the saying that everything had a place. If he walked to the kitchen and found tweezers on the counter, he would say, "Lisa, go put these away."

And I would say, "Dad, I don't know where they go."

And he would say, "Find a place. Everything has a place, so find a place."

My mom was organized as well, but the complexities of her life, multiple responsibilities, and passions created a few disordered spaces and times of life for her. As an artist and a home-based business owner, her life was full, sometimes to the point of overflowing. But she was really good at keeping all the stuff that was going on in a contained space.

She ran her business from our basement, selling a seasonal clothing line through reps in twenty-five states. She would go to New York, buy the clothing, and have it shipped to our house. Once the clothing arrived, she sorted it into sets to be shipped in cases to each rep's home for an in-home showing. After one or two weeks, the reps would send their orders to my mom and ship the case of clothing to the next rep in line.

As you can imagine, there was clothing everywhere in our basement. My mom had a few employees as well, and the basement was a fun, productive place to be.

I was in grade school when my mom started this business. I loved being able to work for her. My favorite job was taking all the checks and storing them by check number. We also alphabetized invoices.

I would take a stack of invoices upstairs to the family room. My mother had used masking tape on a wooden lapboard to help sort the invoices: A-E, F-J, K-M, N-R, S-T, U-Z. I thought it was so cool to sort those while the TV was on!

One summer I was bored. My own room was clean, and there was no area in the main part of the house that I could organize without my mom's supervision. In our basement, there was a workbench in the furnace room. It was a large, L-shaped, built-in workbench with shelves above it. There were some art supplies in there, vases, all of the gift-wrap stuff, wallpaper, and other odds and ends that came with the house we'd moved into eight years prior. It was just a junk collector. No one really went in there except to get gift wrapping supplies.

I went into that furnace room and decided I was going to surprise my mom and organize that space. There was a whole bunch of stuff that had been there forever that I knew could be gotten rid of. So I put it in a pile to say, "I think you should get rid of this, Mom." (I have never gotten rid of things without telling people.)

Then I cleaned the space. The furnace room was dusty and grimy, which is another reason why we didn't use that space much. After I moved out the old stuff and cleaned the space, I looked at what was left. I sorted like items together and I organized it.

In the end, all the vases were in one place, all the paint was in one place, and all the gift wrap was organized. I couldn't wait to show my mom. She was so surprised. She quickly looked over the organized space and pulled out more items we could get rid of. After that, the family started actually using that space to wrap gifts. The space got more and more organized over time because I would continue to organize it and refine the space's use.

Babysitting and Organizing

The day I turned twelve, I took the Red Cross babysitting course and started to look for babysitting jobs. A few months later, I spent a lot of time at our local pool, playing with toddlers and collecting new clients.

All through high school, I babysat for doctors' families. It was very common for the couple to be out until eleven or twelve, sometimes even one o'clock in the morning. I babysat most weekends from the time I was twelve until I was eighteen.

One of the first families that I babysat for had an eight-year-old and a toddler. Often I would babysit both of them. I loved that, because it was a challenge for me to see how I could entertain these two very different age groups at the same time.

Playing with the kids was fun, but I got bored after they went to bed. Especially when the eight-year-old was at an overnight and I just had the baby. The baby would go to bed between seven and nine, and I would be at the house until twelve or one.

At first, it was great to eat junk food and watch TV, but eventually that got old. One night, I went to the pantry to get something to eat, and I lingered there. It was a floor-to-ceiling cabinet pantry. I opened both sides and looked at the lower shelves. There were four or five shelves that were two feet deep and filled with food and crafts.

There were no shoebox sorters in there; it was just all food, craft stuff, and some toys. It was just a hot mess of a pantry, and I wasn't really hungry.

All I could think as I looked at it was that it was like a gigantic puzzle. I would love to organize this. I was trying to talk myself out of it because I felt like I was invading their privacy. I was thinking, "How can I organize their pantry without their permission?" I reasoned that it was probably okay if I organized the kids' art supplies, because that's kid-related, and I was hired to work with the kids.

I took all the art supplies out, and I got that whole shelf all totally beautiful. Then I looked at all the other disorganized shelves. I thought, "I will just do one more shelf." Next thing you know, the whole entire pantry was done. I had a pile of stuff that was expired (I had checked all the dates), and everything left looked fabulous.

I went on and did the bread drawer. Then I said, "Oh my gosh, oh my gosh, oh my gosh. I have totally violated these people's privacy. I have organized. They have not said I can organize. I have this whole pile of trash. What if they want to keep these expired, moldy pieces of bread? I can't believe I did this."

At midnight when the parents come home, I was so excited and nervously said, "I hope it's okay that I organized the pantry." When the mom opened the pantry doors, she was ecstatic. Now, as a mother myself, I can see why she would be ecstatic. She didn't have time to do that. It was great that I did it for her.

My organizing "surprises" have always been met with gratitude, but to this day, I know that organization is a private thing. To go into somebody's space and organize it, you must respect it. You need permission. And you don't want to get rid of any of their stuff, because you don't know what is or isn't important to them.

This parent was very receptive to my desire to organize spaces. One of the games I would play with both her children was hide-and-seek—on all three levels of the house. During one of those games, I was in the laundry room too long, so I organized it. After that, the mom said to me, "You know, you're allowed to organize the kid's rooms." I couldn't wait!

The next time I babysat, it was just me and the eight-year-old. I was super excited to play this new game called "Let's Clean Your Room." She was not. I used all the sales tactics I could muster and got started. It took a couple of babysitting sessions, one for the bedroom and another for her closet. But it was really fun. I had turned it into a game, and she actually liked it. The mom was thrilled!

At that time, I babysat for four families. A couple of the other families started allowing me to organize as well. I would ask, "Is it all right if I organize your pantry when the kids have a nap?" And they said, "Um, yeah." Like, why would that not be okay? So I would babysit AND I would organize.

I was having a great time playing babysitter and housekeeper with these four families. I would organize kitchens, organize kid stuff, and babysit the kids. My desire to play house was insatiable. It was all I wanted to do.

I was a very entrepreneurial child, and I did not want to get a traditional job. So when summertime came, I would call these mothers and I would say, "You really need me to come one day a week so you can go get your hair done and play golf and go out to lunch with your friends. I'll take the kids to swim lessons, and here and there and everywhere, and that will be your day." This mom had Tuesday, that mom had Wednesday, and another mom had Mondays and Fridays.

I would take care of the kids and organize the house. Of course, I never did any cooking. The kids would say I burned grilled cheese, which was absolutely true!

One of those moms had four children. When I was in high school, I babysat for this family two, sometimes three, days a week. I also went on vacations with them. That mom was the first person to hire me to wrap Christmas presents. She was very receptive to any and all organization I wanted to do as well.

Learning to Design Spaces

They had a fifth child when I was in college, a girl.

While I was away, they transitioned the space above their three-car garage into a big bedroom for their two girls. But to get to that new bedroom, you had to walk through the bedroom that used to be the older daughter's. That winter break when I came home from college, the mom asked me, "How do we do this? We have a preteen daughter and we have a baby. How do we organize this space?"

I went up there with her and walked in and out of both rooms, looking at the two closets, the configuration of the spaces, and analyzing it all. The bedrooms and closet construction had been completed, but the bedroom furniture had not been moved in yet.

Here is what the space looked like as you walked into the old bedroom. To the right was a door to a walk-in closet that ran the length of the old bedroom. It was under the roof line, so one side of the closet held only short-hanging clothes. Straight ahead was the door to the new bedroom and to the left was the old bedroom space. Off the left wall was an entrance to a Jack and Jill bathroom the girls would share with a brother.

The new bedroom was the size of a three-car garage. As you walked into the space, one car could fit to the right and two cars could fit on the left. Centered on the far wall were two dormers with windows. There was a closet to the left just as you entered the room.

I walked into and out of the new bedroom, imagining where to put all the furniture and how to divide the space. I was giddy with the possible combinations and so excited for the girls.

I suggested they think about the old bedroom as the preteen's dressing room. That way, as the baby grew into a toddler, the teenager would have a space to get ready and keep her clothes and possessions tucked away. In the old bedroom space, she would have access to the new bedroom, the bathroom, and the old closet.

Then she could just sneak into the bedroom and go to bed at night.

In the new space, I suggested locating the baby's bedroom space on the right side. A crib and changing table do not take up much space. That would give the teenager a larger bedroom space. We also talked about giving each of the children one of the dormers as mini-private spaces. The older child's became a reading nook and the baby's held a play kitchen.

I remember that conversation like it was yesterday. Here I was, maybe eighteen or nineteen at the time, consulting with a mother who had five children about how to organize her kids' bedrooms and closets. I knew I had the answer.

Organizing a Craft Space

At the same time, my parents had redone part of their house. My dad had bumped out our two-and-a-half-car garage so it was now a five-car garage. In the back of the garage, my dad created a large craft room for my mom. Our house was built in 1958 and had a heated garage, so it was okay to create a living space out there.

My mom finally had a space where she could create to her heart's content. The room was the size of a small galley kitchen with counters all the way around on every single wall. The counters made a big U shape, with a single row of drawers below the counter. It was open enough underneath to allow for storage bins, chairs, or rolling totes. The flooring was made of recycled tires. You could vacuum it if you wanted to or you could spray it down with a hose.

Different people organize differently. I told you earlier that my father always said there's a place for everything. Well, my mom is a very visual learner, and she's an artist. For some artists to get inspiration, they need to be surrounded by stuff. They get inspiration and ideas from anything. A little tiny scrap of red paper that you think is trash is not trash because that is the perfect red. They're still trying to match that red, or that is going to be Rudolph's nose on twelve different cards. But you don't realize that little scrap of paper can be made into that many Rudolph noses.

I knew that all the stuff my dad saw as clutter, my mom saw as treasures. I was fascinated by how they could both be so successful in their work and yet be so different in how they used their physical spaces.

One day, my dad went into my mom's craft room while she was gone and he "cleaned" it for her. When she came back, the craft room looked amazing. He had wiped down all the counters with Windex. He even vacuumed the floor. Of course, my mom's first question was, "Where is my stuff?" Well, it was in a Hefty bag because it all looked like trash to my dad. She was so mad.

I remember observing that exchange, seeing that my dad wanted order in the room even though he had closed it off from the rest of the house (so it was allowed to be messy). He desired for it to be organized. My mom liked it when it was organized, but she needed all of her stuff.

So, over the next year and a half, I would organize that room with my mom, with the goal of achieving the order my dad wanted and the storage for all of the stuff that my mom wanted.

When I started, I began by not touching a thing. I would sit in the room and ask a million questions about every piece of paper, every stamp, every envelope, everything. "Why are you keeping it? How often do you need it? Where do you use it?"

Mom was pretty patient with my questions, because she too desired that the room "look good," but she also wanted to know where her stuff was. She needed a system to put things away at the end of a long crafting session or when a project was complete.

The first time we organized that room together, it took us a couple of days. Four months later when I came home from college, we organized the space again. This time we got it done in a day. Six months later, we did it again in about six hours.

On the next visit home, my mom went out on an errand and I went into her craft room by myself to surprise her. I organized it in three hours. When she came home, everything was put away. She loved it. My dad loved it because it looked organized. She loved it because all of her stuff was still there and she knew where it was.

Organizing a crafting space is the most labor-intensive professional organizing that I do. First, there is just a lot of stuff! Craft items take a long time to organize. Second, each creative person uses their crafts differently, and you need to understand the purpose of the supplies and the creative process of the artist to get it right. Most creative people can maintain organization, but they have a hard time creating organization in their craft areas. In working with my mother that year, I earned a PhD in organization.

I always go back to that story because that's where I truly learned how to organize. Helping my mom organize the craft room was when I actually organized for someone with them, for their purposes. When I was organizing the pantries for the families I babysat for, they really didn't care if I changed where the cereal was, as long as I kept putting it back in the same place. I was allowed to create the order. When I was organizing the furnace room, no one really used that room. I was really just organizing junk that was eventually going to be discarded. Nobody loved that stuff.

But my mom's craft room was her passion. That was her outlet. That was her. To be able to organize to her and Dad's levels of satisfaction really taught me a lot of the skills that I still use today.

So often in my in-home professional organization consultations, I am really helping each client see that they CAN live a more organized life. I am listening for clues: what has worked in the past, what is working now, and how they use the space. Often, these consultations require reassuring the husband and the wife that the space will be organized with both function and aesthetic concerns in mind.

As my childhood and adolescent years came to an end, I had yet to experience a time when I myself was unorganized. Oh, my time was coming . . . and soon!

In the next section, we'll look at the organizational skills that are learned in childhood.

ORGANIZING A CHILD'S BEDROOM

I will not organize a young lady's bedroom with her mom there. With that in mind, this section is written to the young lady who is between seven and twenty-one years old.

This is just a time for me to organize with you, not with your mom. We're not going to think about Mom most of the time when we're organizing this room.

Let's start with a dose of reality. Whatever size your bedroom is—if it's small, if it's big, if it has a bathroom attached—there's nothing you can do to change that. You can wish it was bigger. You can wish you had a bathroom. But the fact remains, your bedroom is the size that it is.

<u>The first step in getting organized is not wishing that you had something bigger or something better.</u> My husband and daughter watch iCarly all the time, and she has an amazing bedroom. So I hear about this bedroom all the time. Well, that is TV; that is not realistic. I don't know anybody who has a bedroom like that. I want you to come to terms with, "Okay, this is my bedroom. I can't change this until I have my own house."

But I also want you to be empowered by your bedroom. I want you to view your bedroom like it is your own mini-apartment. Because it is; it's your very own space inside of your parents' house. No matter what size your bedroom is, you will be able to do everything that I am going to tell you in this chapter.

If your parents are anything like me, they're always saying, "You can't eat that. You can't put that there. No, you can't take the dog for a walk at night." All these things I'm telling my kids they can't do. But when it comes to your bedroom, you can probably do almost anything you want. It's your responsibility to clean it and organize it. If you think about your bedroom as *your* space, you will start to take better care of it, and you'll really enjoy your bedroom.

There are four basic steps to organizing your room. Steps that you're going to do every single week.

Step 1 — Pick a day and time weekly to clean and organize your room.

There really is no way around this one. You need to clean and organize your room every week. If you skip a week, the clutter gets so out of control, it is really hard to get it done without being overwhelmed and frustrated.

The most natural time to organize your bedroom, unless you have a sporting event, is Saturday morning. Come home on Friday, ride your bike, go out, do whatever you want. Then Saturday morning, when you get up, turn on some fun music and organize your room.

At first, it may take you two to four hours to clean and organize your room. But after four weeks, it will get quicker and easier. Eventually, you should be able to get your whole room clean and organized in an hour or less.

Some kids come home from school and they clean and organize their room on Friday so they can enjoy it organized all weekend. Some put it off until Sunday afternoon before the school week starts because they procrastinate and they don't want to do it.

Here's a hint . . . procrastinating is not going to make the task of organizing your room go away, so just do it. Easy for me to say, right? I like to organize my room. But I'm telling you, after you learn about how to get your room the way you want it, you will actually enjoy organizing, too!

What I have learned over time is that everyone can be organized. Some people just have to learn how to do it.

If you leave your room messy and refuse to clean it and you don't want to learn how to get organized, you're going to grow up and have an apartment that you're then going to have to learn how to organize. It's going to be much harder to learn to be organized as an adult than it is at your age. You're going to have to learn this sometime, so you might as well learn it now.

Step 2 – Do the top three tasks: Clean up trash and food, take out all the dirty laundry, and clean up your floor.

Each week, no matter what, start by doing these three things first:

1. Pick up all the trash, and put anything food related back in the kitchen.
2. Pick up all the dirty clothes, and put them in the hamper or laundry room.
3. Pick up and put away what is on your floor.

Step 1 is to get a new trash bag and empty out your trashcan. Look around the room, and get all of the food and all of the trash out. If you're in charge of the bathroom, empty the bathroom trash, too. Tie the trash bag up, take it downstairs, and put it in the trashcan in the garage.

Next, take any food that you brought into your bedroom back to the kitchen for the whole family. So now there is no food and no trash in your bedroom.

Step 2 is to collect all of those dirty clothes that are all over the place and put them in the laundry room, if your mom still does the laundry. If you do your own laundry, start a load.

If your mom stores the hangers in the laundry room, take all of the empty hangers out of your closet and put them in the laundry room so they are there to hang up the clothes again.

Step 3 is to pick up everything on the floor. This is usually where your school supplies, backpack, books that you've been looking at, toys you've been playing with, and makeup are. Clean up the floor so that you can run the vacuum.

Step 3 — Look around and see if there is anything you can donate or get rid of.

I am going to be encouraging you to get rid of stuff. Here's why . . .

- Your room is not a house. You have limited space to store your treasures, and you need to make sure they are still treasures and not just old stuff you don't know what to do with.
- You are always getting new stuff, which means you need to get rid of old stuff.
- Things break, you lose pieces, and you just stop playing with stuff over time.

The only way to get your room more organized is to get rid of stuff. I did this for years and years and years with my daughter. Eventually, she realized that the more she got rid of, the less I was in her room organizing it. There wasn't as much stuff to organize, and she was able to start organizing her own room.

So how do you do this?

1. Decide what you no longer play with or want.
2. Take it to your mom, and see if she or your siblings want it.
3. Help mom create a donation box or basket where you can put stuff that you no longer want.

Look around the room and think, "Okay, what is in this room that I don't really want anymore?"

Let's say that you are into Barbies now and you used to be into Polly Pockets, and both of them are in your bedroom. You agree with me, you're not going to play Polly Pockets anymore, but you're not really ready to give them away.

Then you can take all of those Polly Pockets, put them in a box or Ziploc bag, and hand them to your mom and say, "I don't want to get rid of these, but I don't want to play with them right now," and she will put them in the storage room or the closet or somewhere else in the house.

Or you can just donate them. Now, this is super hard for adults, and I know it's going to be hard for you, too. But eventually, we just have to learn how to give our stuff away. Yeah, we love the stuff that we get, and we love to play with it, but eventually we're done with it.

Say your mom took you out and said, "Okay, we're going to go out to fast food. You can pick any restaurant you want." You go and you get whatever you love and you eat it. It's yummy and it's all gone.

Are you going to keep the wrapper that the food came in because you loved going out to that fast food restaurant with your mom? No. You've already eaten the food. It's gone. It's in your belly. So you don't need to have the container anymore, because you had the experience with your mom.

The same thing happens with your stuff. Let's say you played Polly Pockets for three or four years straight. You played it with your best friend, and you have so many great memories of playing Polly Pockets and the inventive games that you created on long summer nights. Or the week that you were sick and your mom played Polly Pockets with you.

You have all these memories attached to Polly Pockets, but you're fifteen and there are still Polly Pockets in your bedroom. You love all of the memories you have of playing with Polly Pockets, but are you going to play with Polly Pockets again? No, you're not going to play with Polly Pockets again. Even if your best friend comes over, or you're sick for a week, you're not going to play Polly Pockets again, right?

You're done with Polly Pockets, so it's okay to give them away. Because number one, you still have the memories; you don't have to keep the stuff. And number two, wouldn't it be awesome if you put all your Polly Pockets stuff in a Ziploc bag and gave it away, and then some other little girl got that Ziploc bag of Polly Pockets stuff and she got to create all those awesome memories like the ones you created? Wouldn't that be great?

Don't think of getting rid of things as getting rid of memories. You get to keep the memories. Not only that; you get to give the opportunity for somebody else to make the same awesome memories.

I just want to say real quickly: If you're anything like me . . . if I was a kid and somebody had told me that, I would have gone in my bedroom and given everything away because I would have wanted everyone to have more memories. That's not what I'm saying. Do not give away the toys that you currently play with or the passions that you currently have.

Let's say you play with Polly Pockets, but this week you're not playing with them. You're not ready to get rid of them yet. You don't donate them until you haven't played with them for probably a year. So anything in your bedroom that you haven't played with for a full year, you can probably get rid of.

When you're ready to get rid of something, you first have to take it to your mom and say, "Hey, mom. I don't want to play Polly Pockets anymore." And ask your brothers and sisters, "I don't want the Polly Pockets anymore, does anybody else want the Polly Pockets?"

You may have a sibling that says, "Oh, I want all the Polly Pockets." Great! They're not going to be in your bedroom anymore; they're going to be in their bedroom. Or your mom may say, "Oh, I love the Polly Pockets. Remember when we played Polly Pockets when you were sick that week? Oh, that was so great." Then your mom can keep the Polly Pockets as a memory for herself somewhere else in the house.

Now this is super hard for both your mom and for you. And this is why I don't let moms organize in bedrooms when I organize with their kids. You have memories with Polly Pockets and your mom has memories with Polly Pockets as well, but the memory is really in your heart—it's not in the actual Polly Pockets. Some people have a really hard time getting rid of the Polly Pockets and keeping the memory in their heart without actually holding the Polly Pockets. And if your mom has a hard time, then she'll keep the Polly Pockets, and that's fine. She owns the whole entire house, remember? So she can keep them somewhere else in the house because it's her whole entire house. But you only have your bedroom, your little apartment. That's where you keep everything.

If you don't want to play with the Polly Pockets anymore, but you don't feel ready to give them away, then you can put them in a bag, and you can either put them under your bed or in your closet. Don't feel like you need to get rid of them if you want to keep them and the memory at the same time. I'm going to keep talking in this book about how the skill of letting go of things but keeping the memory is a really hard thing to learn. Some people do it easier than others.

Look around the room and see if there's anything you're finished with that you're ready to donate. That might be a book, it might be some clothing, it might be a toy. It doesn't have to be a lot of things. I'm going to encourage you to find ten things to donate, only ten. It could be ten books, ten shirts, or whatever the easiest thing is for you to let go. And if that was super, super easy, then give away ten more. Do a total of twenty.

Step 4 — Clean. That means vacuum and dust!

Ahem, yes. Cleaning means CLEANing. Once you have your room organized, run the vacuum and dust your dresser. NOTE: For safety, please wear tennis shoes or shoes where your toes are covered when you vacuum.

Bedroom Organization Recap:

1. You need to pick a day and time WEEKLY to clean and organize your room.
2. Do the top three tasks: Clean up trash and food, take out all the dirty laundry, and clean up your floor.
3. Look around and see if there is anything you can donate or get rid of.
4. Clean. That means vacuum and dust!

Download the kids' bedroom cleaning checklist and get links to more bedroom organizing ideas at www.organize365.com/book-bonus.

How do you know what to save from your childhood, and what is the best way to preserve those memories? Let's take a look.

SAVING YOUR CHILDREN'S MEMORABILIA

Once the room is clean and organized, the physical reminders of childhood memories often end up in Mom's storage room—usually indefinitely. So, Mom, what are we going to do with all those treasures in your attic and basement?

For years, I just "organized" my piles into cuter containers, better systems, and a larger house. But organization is not about containers or beautiful systems. It is about keeping what you want and love so you can enjoy those items now and in the future.

I wasn't really purging. I wasn't really getting rid of anything. I was just making everything look better, but I was saving it all.

Once I had kids, I realized that if I kept saving everything, we would quickly outgrow the house. Even though we bought our house before we had kids, it is our forever home. Now that I've really been purging things and thinking more about what I like, want, and need, we actually have a lot of empty cabinets, empty closets, and extra space, which is really weird and really fun.

A long time ago, I used to listen to this podcast called *Clutter Interrupted*. One of the things that Professional Organizer Tracy Hoth would often say is that clutter is delayed decision-making. I find myself saying that to my clients all the time.

When you get to your storage room, you naturally think about memories. It's where people who otherwise have their whole house organized still do not feel organized because they are delaying making decisions, resulting in clutter. Now I'm going to give a caveat.

I've mentioned before that it seems to take about five years to get through certain stages in life. Five years to the day after my mother-in-law had her stroke, it's like a light switch went on in her brain and she could remember and do things she hadn't been able to do for five years. Five years after my father passed away, it seemed like different things in the family were clicking again and everyone had processed the change of losing him and all the different relationships that he had.

Five years seems to be the amount of time it takes to really process things. So I'm going to give you some hard-and-fast rules about how to get rid of stuff, but I want you to hear me first. If you are going through a tragedy or you've just lost a spouse or your children have just gone away to college or moved out of the country—if some big event is going on, don't just say, "Well, Lisa says to get rid of it all." No, I'm talking about after it's been five years, when you're ready to tackle this clutter—that's when I want you to implement these strategies.

Think about your kids' stuff. Whether your kids are two years old, twenty-two years old, forty-two years old, or sixty-two years old, it doesn't matter. I want you to think about your kids as we look at their stuff that you have kept. What do they want to keep? What do you want to keep? And when do you each want this stuff?

What Do Your Kids Want to Keep?

I had to come to grips with the fact that we were not going to keep all of the stuffed animals that came into our house. I would try everything I could to have people not give my kids stuffed animals because once they got into our home, I found it was harder for me to get rid of them than it was for my kids.

And at one point, we had a lot of stuffed animals. When the kids were three and four years old, I put all of the stuffed animals in the middle of the room. There were over a hundred! I divided them up by type. All the Clifford dogs went together, all the bears went together, all the frogs went together. And I said to the kids, "You know, we need to give some of these to other people. Which ones can we get rid of?" They were giving me lots of animals and I would say, "Well, could you give me two more?" I was pushing them to the point where they were giving up everything they wanted to give up, and everything that was left, they really, really wanted.

But some of the stuffed animals they gave up, I tried to convince them to keep. "Why do you want to give up Clifford the Big Red Dog? You got that when Abby was born, you know."

Joey looked at me, and I stopped. He had picked four other Clifford the Big Red Dogs that he didn't want to give up. Now, I had created guilt in a four-year-old, telling him he should keep a fifth Clifford the Big Red Dog. I thought, "Oh my gosh. If I keep doing this, we're going to outgrow this house before the kids go to kindergarten. This is not going to work."

From that day forward, whenever the kids were ready to get rid of anything, I let them. Unless it was super, super sentimental; then, I did store it in the basement. But I can think of only maybe three occasions when the kids were ready to give up something and I actually kept it for them, thinking that, you know what, they might really want this object in the future.

I want to shift your perspective. Imagine that your mother has just shown up to your house, and she is going to be giving you every single school paper you have ever written on, every stuffed animal you ever had, all the clothes you wore for the first three years of your life, and every toy you touched before the age of twelve. Are you overwhelmed?

Okay, I know. First, you might be thinking, "That'd be really cool. I'd love to see what I played with when I was ten," or "I was always wondering how I did on spelling tests." There is a little piece of us that thinks, "Oh, that'd be really cool to see all my history."

But after you get over that blip of "that would be really cool," can you really imagine a U-Haul showing up with all this stuff? Then you'd have to process it and decide what you were going to do with it, right? Honestly, you really don't want all of the things from your childhood.

Let's think about what your kids really want. When they're ready to get rid of things, go ahead and let them get rid of things. They are going through the normal purging/saving process. And even though you want to save everything they've done under your roof because it's a memory and something you cherish and want to remember, they are processing through life. You wouldn't save every single thing you bought from the time you were twenty to fifty, right? So why should you save every single thing that you owned from the time you were five to eighteen? You shouldn't.

Each child will have a different way that they want to process their things. My daughter will easily get rid of things after a couple of months. They never go into storage. Once she's done with them, she's done with them. I can send them off to Goodwill right away.

My son has fewer possessions, and he is more sentimental. When he wants to get rid of things, he'll have a certain amount that he gets rid of right away. "Okay, don't need that." But then he'll have this other pile of stuff that he will not be ready to get rid of, but that he no longer wants in his room. This tells me it's on its way out, but he wants some more processing time. So, I box up those things and put them in the basement. Then when we go through his room and organize it a couple times a year, I'll remind him what's in the basement.

The last time we organized his room together, I reminded him about what I had in the basement. "Do you want all those train tracks, matchbox cars, and plastic car tracks?"

He said, "You still have all that?"

And I said, "Yeah."

For a minute, he was nostalgic, just like you would be if your mom said she still had everything you had when you were kid. And then he said to me, "I didn't even know that was down there. Get rid of it and don't tell me. If I start looking at all that, I'm going to want to keep it. But if you just get rid of it, I won't even care."

For the record, neither of my children have ever said, "Mom, where is x-y-z, I want to see that." Since they have a say in what gets kept or donated, they have no regrets about the items that are donated. We often think our children will ask us for an object from their past, but in my experience, they don't.

So think about that. Are you setting your kids up for success in the future by helping them process and get rid of things that they are done with now? What do they really want to keep? Do they want to keep every single trophy they've ever had? Or would they like to only keep their two first place trophies and have you take pictures of the rest? Kids will get rid of more than you think, if you do the heavy lifting.

What Do You Want?

You might want more of your child's mementos than they do. You might want to keep their baby clothes, baby toys, and their American Girl doll collection long after they're done with them.

There are couple reasons for this. Number one, you spent the money. They didn't, right? It's a significant amount of cha-ching going out the door every time they're done with something that maybe you just bought a few months earlier. I often hear myself saying, "Are you kidding me? You're done with this already?"

But I think more to the point, and I know this to be true for me, it's that I really enjoyed that stage of my child's life. I really enjoyed the Duplo blocks building stage. I really enjoyed the little table that the kids could barely stand at and how Abby imitated me when she held her toy phone.

That toy was only used for maybe eight months, and then they were done with it. It doesn't matter how long I save it; they will never play with it again. But I love those memories of them, and seeing that toy in the storage room reminds me of all of those times.

It's not going to remind your child of all those times. When they have their children, they're going to want their own toys. So the real question is when they have their own children. Do you want to still have that toy at your house so when they come to visit, you have it for them to play with? In that case, have at it. Save as much as you want. However, think about how you were with your own children.

I went shopping constantly for my children. I'd waited for those babies so long that I was at the store all the time. Joey liked to be out of the house and he was perfectly happy sitting in a stroller going through Walmart.

I'm ashamed to admit that we were at Walmart pretty much every day at 8:01 a.m. We had toys everywhere. Then I would go to garage sales and buy toys. And I would have garage sales and sell toys. I was managing toy organization all over the house and I loved it.

When we have grandchildren, do you think I'm not going to go to a store? I know kids stay in toy phases for only three, six, or nine months at a time, and then they're on to something else. So I have saved maybe three toys for future grandbabies. Because I realize that even though I loved playing with those toys with my kids and I could totally see myself playing with those toys with my grandchildren, I don't even know if I'll have grandchildren. Maybe my kids won't have kids, or maybe they'll have kids when they're forty, which is still another twenty-five years from now. Who knows what the toys will be like then, right? Or even where I will be living then. So, I went ahead and got rid of the toys.

But if you want to keep them, save them for yourself. Let's say your kids are teenagers. They're not very sentimental kids, but you're very sentimental. As you're sorting through your storage room treasures, I want you to box things up based on who wants it. If your child wants all of their trophies (but they don't want them in their room) and you don't want them either, then I want you to box them up in a banker's box and label it "Suzy Q's Trophies." So you can look at that box and say, "Okay, those are Suzy Q's, they're not for me." Or when you're boxing up baby clothes, you pick maybe two or three that you're saving to give your daughter when she has her first child. "Hey, this is what you wore. Isn't this fun?" And you get rid of all of the rest.

Here is where I'm going with these labeled boxes. Depending on where you are in your phases of life, when you get to about fifty-five to sixty and the kids are off to college, or the last one flies away from the nest, you will look around your home and say, "Yes, it's finally quiet and it's all mine."

You love your kids and you want them to come back, but (I haven't been there yet, so I'm just imagining) there's a sense of thinking, if I turn the light off, it's going to stay off. If I buy yogurt and put it in the refrigerator, it's going to be there the next day. If I put my scissors down on the counter, they will still be there when I come back. You're getting your house back.

That is when you're going to look at all the stuff in the storage room and think, "Why do we have all of her trophies? Really? Does she really want her trophies?" And you're going to get the urge to purge things that maybe you shouldn't purge because they're hers.

That's when I recommend getting a storage unit. And if the boxes are all already labeled, then you can easily move them right out of your house.

Then you can move, maybe even downsize to a patio home, but your child's mementos are still safely stored and waiting for them.

When Do You Want It?

Now, I want to talk to you about when you each want these items. Because not only are we delaying decision-making by putting a whole bunch of stuff in our storage room; we also can't enjoy all that stuff we're keeping. We constantly feel guilty, thinking, "It's all down there, I need to organize it. It's all down there, I need to do something with it."

You can't enjoy your child's baby clothes in a box in your storage room. Your child can't enjoy their trophies in a box somewhere. This is why I love scrapbooks. Even though it takes so much time to figure out which pictures you want and to arrange them all. Whether they use digital or traditionally printed pictures, scrapbooks are awesome. I cannot even tell you how many times my kids look at their scrapbooks.

The same thing is true with the school binders. You could save bin after bin after bin of kids' school papers, but who's looking at them, and who's enjoying them, and what good is that? But if you take the time to put the best ones in a binder, you and your kids can easily flip through and enjoy the progress they have made.

My kids look at their school binders a few times a year. They love their school binders, but they never would have gone into a storage room and gone through boxes of paper to find the handprint that they made into a turkey. You know what I'm saying?

Using the following memory-saving process, you will be able to empty your storage room and relive your favorite memories.

The Memory-Saving Process

1. Process through the piles.
2. Pick the best.
3. Experience the memories together.
4. Enjoy a new creation.
5. Empty out your storage room without emptying out your heart.

In the next chapter, you will read all about how Greg and I became parents in the blink of an eye through adoption. The night we picked up Joey, I remember Greg laying this little baby on our bed and just kneeling and looking at him, while I ran around and did everything we needed to do in order to go to bed. The next morning, we both drove to Walmart and we got Joey some clothes, because he was really little and he needed the preemie size.

How did I know that Walmart had a great preemie selection even before I had kids? I used to talk about children so much that my father named my future children Inviso 1 and Inviso 2. He would say, "How are the Invisos doing, Lisa?" Because we didn't have babies, but I just talked about them all the time. I am a baby nut! But you should know, I don't have any of their baby clothes saved except the outfits they came to us in.

Early on, I was saving all of Joey's baby clothes for future children. Eighteen months later, we adopted his little sister. I wasn't sure if we were going to have any more babies, but it didn't make any sense to save all the boy baby clothes and all the girl baby clothes. What if the next baby was a boy born in a different season? For Joey's second birthday, I took all the baby clothes I had saved and used my favorites to make a patchwork quilt.

Now, I'm not a great sewer, but I had sewed some baby sleepers and a few bibs for my kids. They weren't perfect, but they were fun. I thought, "Okay, I'll take their clothes, and I'll turn them into a baby blanket."

Every little piece of clothing had a memory. There were all those little baby clothes that Greg and I got the first day that we had Joey. There was the layette my grandmother sent down, a collection of gorgeous outfits from department stores. They were the kind of baby clothes you would have bought in a time gone by. I also included some of my favorite soft sleepers.

Let me show you how I went through the memory-saving process with my kids' baby clothes.

Step 1 — Process through the piles.

I decided that I would make a blanket. I made a three-by-three-inch square template out of cardboard. Then, I started cutting all the baby clothes into three-by-three-inch squares that I wanted to save.

I thought this blanket might replace those little waffle-textured blankets Joey carried around, and I cut some of those blankets into nine-by-nine-inch segments for the back. I wasn't sure how Joey would respond. But I knew that I didn't want to save all these clothes. I knew I wanted to make a memory. I knew I wanted something that we could experience now, not just a bunch of baby clothes in boxes.

Step 2 — Pick the best.

Since Joey had such horrible reflux, some of my favorite outfits were ruined by spit up, but they still had a few good pieces in them. I picked fourteen outfits that I thought, "These are the ones I want to tell him about. These are the ones I want to save the memory of."

Step 3 — Experience the memories together.

When I made the kids' school binders, they got to experience the memories with me. I made the books, and then we sat down and went through them page by page together. I got to see their faces, hear their stories about these papers I didn't even know much about. It was just really a great bonding experience.

With this baby blanket, it was Greg and me who got to experience the memories together. When he would come home from work at night, I would be cutting all these baby clothes apart and we would reminisce: "You remember this outfit that we bought?" And Greg would tell a story about something Joey did in that outfit.

We were able to experience the memories of those baby clothes, the memories of becoming parents for the first time, the memories of being parents of two babies. That's what we were experiencing, not the clothing. The clothing was just the conduit to the conversation, you see.

We enjoyed this process of creation, and Greg and I loved the finished blanket. I had no idea if Joey would like it or not, if he would want to keep it when he was older or not, if he would be a sentimental kid or not. But I knew one thing: I wanted this blanket. If he wants it, it's his. But if he doesn't want it, I would love it. And I would love to have a grandbaby someday, sleeping underneath or on top of this little blanket at my house.

Step 4 — Enjoy the new creation.

We gave Joey the blanket when he turned two, and he adored it. After he opened the present, he put it on the floor, laid on it, and rolled around on it. He carried it around for years.

The same thing happened when we gave Abby her blanket. Now, of course, she knew Joey had a big boy blanket. Even though she was only two, somehow she knew she was getting a big girl blanket too. She carried hers around just as much, and probably even longer. Now they're both in the storage room.

They do come out on occasion. It's kind of funny, but the kids do love those blankets. They have so much meaning for them, and of course, I made a scrapbook page about it. On the scrapbook page, there's a picture of each kid's blanket. I used a Sharpie to number each of the squares in the quilt, and then I wrote where those baby clothes came from, who gave them to the kids, and when they got them, to preserve the memory that goes along with the blanket.

Step 5 — Empty out your storage room without emptying out your heart.

Hopefully after you hear that story, you think, "Oh my gosh, it's so awesome." You have no baby clothes in your closet or your storage room; you just have these two great blankets and the scrapbook page. Some of you are thinking, "Well, great, Lisa. You just added another forty-eight-hour project to my list. Now I've got to make baby blankets out of kids' clothes." I'm not saying you have to make baby blankets out of your kid's clothes. Please do not go on a Pinterest rabbit trail here.

What I am saying is, let's start thinking about how you can take these memories and experiences and continue to enjoy them by creating new things that are visible on a regular basis. My kids see those blankets, they see their school albums, and they see their photo albums.

How can you be enjoying these memories today instead of feeling guilty about where they are tomorrow? It's a worthwhile investment of time. Who's going to do it if you don't? What would you rather give your children, a baby blanket or a whole box full of clothes?

The only baby clothes that I've kept are the little outfits that both kids came to us in when we adopted them. And then, when they have kids, that's what we'll give them.

Maybe the first step for you is to only keep ten to fifteen outfits for each child, and reduce the total number in storage. Make the baby blankets when your children have their first child, or just give them a small collection of clothing.

Now that we've talked about your childhood bedroom and your children's bedrooms, let's move on to the rest of the house.

Phase Two

ACCUMULATION

My Accumulation Story

The accumulation years typically span from age twenty-one to somewhere between thirty-five and forty. These are the years when you are acquiring degrees, a spouse, children, cars, a home, and all the things that go with those milestones.

My accumulation years began in college. I accumulated extra course hours. I went to college every single summer. And I ended up with two degrees when I graduated.

My first year of teaching was a huge learning year for me. I was living on my own in a new city, working in two different buildings, having to share both classrooms with somebody else, and I was creating lots and lots of learning materials. I would draw, color, laminate, and cut out school teaching aids all night long.

In mid-February, I was chatting away with a teacher friend of mine when the regular afternoon bus announcements were interrupted by a familiar male voice. "This message is for Miss Kelly . . . Would you marry me?"

AGHHHHHHH! I ran to the office. Yes!! I was going to be a MRS.! The next summer, we got married, and I became Mrs. Woodruff. All my childhood dreams were coming true.

It had been my goal since birth, or at least as long as I can remember, to be a Mrs. Because with a Mrs. came children, and I was super, super excited to have children. All those years of babysitting were going to pay off!

On our first anniversary, we bought our first house, which we still live in today. I spent a ton of time decorating, wallpapering, and organizing everything in that home. I was preparing our home and our marriage for our future children.

Teaching

Teachers are very, very creative. There are two kinds of teachers that I've come across. The analytical and organized teachers, like me, tend to be the math and science teachers. Then there are the more free-flowing language arts or social studies teachers, who tend to have a lot more stuff in their classrooms. They just love experiential learning. They have lots of ideas and are always going in a million different directions. They would never teach the same lesson the same way twice, because that would be boring.

Not everybody fits that profile, of course, but you will notice that many teachers conform to one of those two categories. When you walk into a classroom, it usually looks organized; after all, classrooms need to be organized for children to learn. It's when you look in each teacher's teacher closet that you can see which kind of teacher you're dealing with.

When I was a student teacher, and in my first years of teaching, my way of socializing with teachers was to go hang out with them in their classrooms. So, of course, when I was hanging out with them, I would say, "Oh, hey, can I organize this paper for you? Can I organize that shelf for you? What if we did something here?" And so I started organizing all the teachers' classroom cabinets. I even organized a few of the teachers' homes just for fun and to hang out.

Lessons in Salesmanship

I joined a direct sales company that sold scrapbook supplies, called Creative Memories. I knew I wanted to work from home like my mom did when I was growing up. It allowed me to have a creative work outlet and the flexibility to be home during the day for my kiddos.

I learned my sales skills from my dad. Specifically, how he got me to eat broccoli. Broccoli is one of my favorite vegetables today and almost always what I order as a side when we go out to eat. But it wasn't always that way. I hated broccoli until my dad told me they were little trees and we covered them in cheese.

He was always a salesperson, selling you the features and the benefits of why this would be great for you and how, if you did it now instead of later, it would be better for you.

It's funny the things you believe as a child. One morning, we were out of milk, and I wanted Rice Krispies cereal. Enter my dad. "Oh, Lisa. Have you ever had them with orange juice?"

"Eww. No, Dad. That's gross."

"No, it's delicious. That's how I always had them growing up." Then my dad poured himself a bowl of Rice Krispies floating in orange juice. He sat down and ate them like it was any other day. And so did I.

This is also how I got talked into eating peanut butter and jelly on a hot dog bun. Now, as a parent myself, I know that he simply didn't want to go to the store. Or we were out of grocery money for the week. Either way, I learned to use what I had available to me at the time, commit to the idea, and have a positive can-do attitude.

I still do that today. I look at the problem at hand, see what tools I have available, and come up with the best solution. I never heard my father complain. He didn't whine about the fact we didn't have milk. He didn't try to decide whose fault it was that the milk ran out. He didn't stock up double on milk the next week. He just solved the problem and moved on.

You know, I don't remember my mother ever complaining either. For dinner growing up, we ate a meat, potato, bread, and vegetable. Sometimes we had nice hot, crispy Pepperidge Farm ciabatta rolls or my favorite flaky Pillsbury croissants for our bread. But I also remember just four slices of bread on a plate and the butter on the table. My favorite bread was when my mom would take hamburger buns, butter them and season them with seasoning salt, and brown them in the oven.

Again, she was probably just trying to use up the old buns, and we might have been out of the regular bread options, but that was my favorite. It is still the one I go to when I need to make a side of bread at our house.

In case you think this only works with food, let me share one more story.

It was a million degrees. Okay, maybe ninety, but the humidity was terrible. I was probably nine or ten years old. Our house did not have air conditioning. My parents had a window air conditioning unit in their bedroom, and on really hot nights, we would sleep on their floor.

I couldn't sleep. It was SO hot. My dad took me back to bed and knelt down next to me. "Okay, Lisa, lay really still. If you lay really still, you will feel the breeze coming in the window."

"I don't feel it, Dad. It's hot."

"Are you laying still? I just felt it. Lay really still. Oh, there—did you feel it?"

"No. Uh, I don't think so."

"Okay. Lay real still. There! Did you feel it?"

"Yeah, Dad! I think I did."

"Okay, good. Just remember, lay really still, and you'll feel the breeze." Years later, he told me there was no breeze, and the window air conditioning unit had broken.

My Home-Based Business

When I joined Creative Memories, I wanted to help families preserve their histories in photo albums for future generations. It was not a hobby. It was a business. I quickly became one of the company's leading salespeople. I replaced my teacher's salary and then some.

My sales strategy was to find women who were committed to preserving their families' histories. I did this mostly through in-home presentations. Unlike my fellow consultants, I did not keep track of the number of parties I hosted or the sales I made. I kept track of the number of people who would buy the "big kit," which consisted of $350 worth of scrapbooking supplies.

I was looking for one hundred customers who I could motivate and encourage, who I could teach to preserve all of their photos and family memories in these albums. I knew that I would find about one client in each party I held.

In my first year in business, I hosted about two to three parties a month, and then for the next ten years, I did about one a month. I preferred to just meet with people one-on-one, introduce them to scrapbooking, and then sell them the big kit.

And I was pretty good at selling those big kits. I always included a free workshop or two with the purchase. My monthly Friday night workshop at my house was where my true business grew. One Friday a month, clients would come and work on their albums for five hours in my basement. We had music, snacks, contests, and a whole lot of fun.

I am very productivity-minded. And I did not want anybody buying this $350 kit and putting it in the bottom of a closet. I wanted them to actually make the albums.

Having over a hundred of these albums myself, and having done more than three hundred for other people, I know how impactful these albums can be. I knew that if I could get my customers to complete their first album, they'd be hooked for life.

For about a year, I had full workshops of eight to ten people, with everyone working on their albums. I saw the productivity of my customers and I thought I had done my job. But really I hadn't, because people had not completed albums yet. They were coming to a workshop on a Friday night and taking five hours to complete three scrapbook pages.

When I became a consultant, I decided I was going to complete one album each month. And I did. I completed an album every month for seven years, the entire time I was a consultant. I always had a complete album at the end of every month. Yet I had not been able to translate what I was doing in my scrapbooking to my customers. I thought I was just faster and each person had their own pace.

Along the way, one of these customers, who was also a teacher, completed an album in just a couple of workshops. I had taught her a strategy called "Power Layouts."

When my client completed that album, not only did her kids give her the positive feedback which I knew would come with a completed album, but she also told the world. She told everybody at her school, everybody in her family, everybody in her neighborhood. She had tons and tons of friends, and she told everybody about this album she made and how I was the one who helped her get it completed. Now I had the recipe to help more clients successfully complete their albums.

Once I had everyone working more productively on their albums, I had less to do. I found myself getting bored. One of my customers said, "Well, you can organize my stuff if you're bored." Yes, please! In that five-hour workshop, I got all of her scrapbooking supplies organized.

At each workshop, another customer would be ready to get organized. Whenever anybody new would come to the workshop and say, "Oh, my stuff is so unorganized," my customers would say, "Lisa, Lisa! So-and-so needs to be organized."

If anyone ever mumbled under their breath, "Where is my paper cutter?" the room would erupt in unison, "Front pocket!" Because everybody's paper cutters were in the same spot in their bag, everybody's stickers were in the same order in their binder, and everybody's paper was in the same order in their paper sorter.

Eventually a client said, "I'd like to hire you to come organize my home."

I thought, "Well, I don't know if I know how to do that."

She said, "We'll just start with the office."

We did the office, then I did a couple of other spaces. Another customer at the workshop and other direct sellers started hiring me to organize their offices as well. I organized both their office spaces and their productivity systems.

Now, mind you, I was not putting these pieces together. I had no idea I was a professional organizer.

Parenthood

Our journey to parenthood did not go according to my plan. It was the first time I set a goal and didn't achieve it on my own timetable. After three years of trying to have a baby, I heard God audibly say to me,

"Lisa, do you want to have a baby or do you want to be a mother?"

I wanted to be a mom.

Four months later, we adopted Joey. And eighteen months later, we adopted Abby.

Joey arrived on a Thursday night. We got the call from the adoption agency around 4:30 p.m., and we were holding Joey in our arms at 7:00. Boom, we were parents.

While I had been preparing my whole life for this event, what we didn't have were supplies. While most parents have baby showers and decorate a nursery, that doesn't always happen with adoptions. All we had was a car seat and the bassinet. The next morning, Greg and I went to the doctor's appointment at 8:00 a.m. and then got a few preemie outfits and some formula at the nearest store before Greg went off to work.

Overnight, I had become a mom. Joey was awesome (just as everybody's baby is), but he also was very colicky. Still to this day, he's not a big sleeper. He is one of the 1 percent of people who can survive on five or six hours of sleep at night.

We, however, wanted him to sleep. I like sleep. Seven to nine hours is usually a good amount for me, and Greg needs eight to nine. Joey didn't nap and didn't really like sleeping at night, either. The poor little guy had reflux and some food sensitivities that we eventually figured out. He cried a lot. He just was not very comfortable.

I am a morning person. So give me the baby in the morning, and I'll take care of him all day. But by 4:00 p.m., I'm exhausted. And by 8:00 p.m., I really want to go to bed. Additionally, whenever there's a transition in my schedule, I find that I tend to sleep more, and I go to bed between 8:00 and 9:00 p.m. until my body adjusts to whatever the new demands are on me.

I'm also a good napper. When Joey would take a catnap in the swing, I would sleep on the couch right next to him and get a twenty- to forty-minute power nap, and that really helped. But by 8:00 p.m., I just could not even function. I was useless.

So Greg would take Joey from 8:00 p.m. to midnight, and then he would try to put him down, and then I would have Joey from 2:00 a.m. on. Joey was awake every two hours for months, but he would sleep from 6:30 a.m. to 10:00 a.m.. So I started sleeping in until 10:00. You have to go with whatever your kid's schedule is at that point just so you can survive.

I remember being so extremely tired at one point that, standing in the shower, I realized I had washed my hair with body soap. And I thought, "Oh, I have to wash my hair again." So I washed my hair again.

I went to rinse it out and realized I had done the same thing. I had put body wash back in my hair again! Now I had to wash my hair for the third time. I chanted out loud in the shower, "Use shampoo! Use shampoo! Use shampoo!" so I would wash my hair with shampoo.

I thought to myself, "What has become of me? I can't even wash my hair anymore?" That's when I realized I was just flat-out exhausted.

However, since we adopted Joey in the middle of the night (literally), I never stopped working. We'd had Joey for only five days when I was holding him and running a meeting for my direct sales company.

I don't know what I was thinking.

With both children, when they turned three months old, I stopped, looked around, and thought, "Oh my gosh, I need to take time off work. I need a little mini maternity leave so I can enjoy these babies."

With each baby, I took about ten days off and really absorbed the fact that our family had grown and my systems needed to change.

Homemaking Expectations

Now I had two things that I loved: These babies that I was dying to be a mother to and this business that was my passion. One night when I went to bed, I prayed that God would not take my direct sales business away from me. I can remember that night so vividly. I so loved being a consultant for this company that I didn't want anything to ever happen to it. I loved working just as I loved having children, but I got to the point where I couldn't necessarily do both. I had these really, really unrealistic expectations in my head of the kind of wife and mother that I would be.

Growing up, we would vacuum our house before my dad got home from work every day. I was doing that for Greg. Every single day, I was vacuuming the house before he got home from work so he would come home to a vacuumed house. Now, as he will tell you, the house does not have to be vacuumed for him. It's nice if it's vacuumed every once in a while, but it's not like it has to be vacuumed every single day.

I also had this unrealistic expectation that I would have these beautiful dinners ready for Greg when he came home. There'd be jazz music playing on the radio, and the children would be all dressed nicely in matching outfits and quietly playing or in their little swings.

When I just had one baby, I was able to meet this unrealistic expectation a couple of times a week. Greg would walk into a clean house, a great dinner on the table, and music on the radio.

In my head, I had such an elaborate picture of this life I would be living. My imaginary house had a picket fence. We didn't have the picket fence. And I imagined myself having four children. We had two. I imagined they would all have matching outfits that they would be dressed in each day.

Growing up, my sister and I would wear matching outfits. My mom even made these matching outfits. So I made my kids' baby clothes! Clearly, it's a good thing I was in my twenties, because I was burning the candle every which way but Sunday. I was making clothes, making meals, working, taking care of children. Looking back at it, I realize it was crazy.

When Abby came along, Joey was a toddler. There were no hot meals and no jazz radio, although the kids did look adorably cute and matched when I could pull that one off. It took me a long time to realize that my expectations and my reality did not line up.

While we were waiting to adopt Abby, I remembered that when I was feeding Joey his bottles, I'd noticed the baseboards were a mess and needed to be painted. Every time I would give him a bottle, I would stare at these baseboards and think, "Oh my gosh. All the baseboards in this house need to be painted." So before we adopted Abby, I painted every single baseboard in our entire house. Then I painted everything else.

I nested like you have no idea. Every single project was done in this house. Everything was clean. I would go out every single day and weed our vegetable garden. Weeds couldn't even grow, because I was weeding so fast. Waiting to adopt Abby, I thought to myself, "I will never be this organized ever again." There was literally not a single thing left in our house to do. I was so ready to have this second child.

Work/Life Balance

My business was growing as fast as the kids. When Joey was a little over two and Abby was around six months, I had just earned a cruise for Greg and me. I really felt like I was in my stride as a mom, but there were things that were getting missed.

There was just so much going on all the time. Joey still wasn't sleeping very much, and he was a bundle of energy. And Abby was adorable and slept great, but when she was awake, she was a little koala bear. She just wanted to be held and loved by Mommy, and of course, I loved doing that. She was my baby, and I love babies, but I just couldn't get it all done.

By the time Abby was born, I already had somebody cleaning our house. I had long since given up on the whole daily vacuuming, dinner, and music ideal. But I didn't want to give up certain things.

I didn't want to give up giving my daughter her nighttime bottle. And I didn't want to give up my Creative Memories business. I also didn't want to give up doing laundry. I liked doing laundry. So I started asking myself what things I wouldn't mind giving up doing, because I wasn't getting everything done. There only so much time.

The first thing I did was hire an assistant to help me with my business for three to five hours a week. My assistant did everything from labeling my catalogs and mailing out mailers to getting my newsletter ready and packaging up orders. She copied fliers, set up displays, and got things ready for my workshop. Anything that I could delegate, she would do.

I could have increased the amount of hours that she was working, but I really didn't have much more that I could delegate. What was left on my list was coaching my downline, coaching my hostesses, coming up with the ideas for the workshops, and preparing presentations—things that I really couldn't delegate.

I realized I was not getting enough work done, but I wasn't getting the home stuff done either. I wasn't getting the bills paid on time. The kids needed a lot of doctor's appointments at that time, and things were getting missed. I constantly felt scattered. At the end of the day, I wasn't able to say I had gotten everything done, and I didn't even know what I was missing. I didn't have a list to tackle the next day. I was so exhausted, I was just falling into bed at night.

This is when I came up with the Sunday Basket System you will read about in the next section.

Even once I got my Sunday Basket System working, it didn't matter how organized I got all my paperwork. There wasn't enough time for me to be a mom, a business owner, and a wife. I couldn't do them all. So Greg and I made the decision to hire a nanny one day a week for ten hours straight. The nanny came at eight on Wednesday morning, and she left at six in the evening.

This was liberating, just life-changing, because I now had a ten-hour block of time when I was supposed to be working.

If you work from home, you may find that you always feel like you're working, but you're never productively working. For example, I would be holding a baby and labeling catalogs at the same time that I was heating up macaroni and cheese. I was multi-tasking everything, and yet I didn't have a definite purpose for any of my time—which left me feeling worn out, but not productive.

When I decided to hire a nanny, Wednesday became my workday. Now everything work-related happened on Wednesdays. I would work from eight to six. Fortunately, I'm one of those people that doesn't need a break. I can work solidly on my business or a job for hours. By the time I was done at six o'clock, I had a nice long list for my assistant when she came on Thursday morning.

Now, of course, I worked other days. I worked a Friday night and maybe a Saturday morning. But once I hired that nanny, I was able to really focus my time. I got more done in those ten hours on Wednesday than I could've gotten done in twenty hours of trying to work and be a mom at the same time.

I want you to realize as you're in this whole baby/toddler stage, it isn't just about you learning to be a mom to these kids. It's also about learning to integrate these kids into your schedule and still keep a part of you.

If you love couponing, maybe you set aside Saturday mornings for two hours to do that. One lady I knew would get up every Saturday morning and go to garage sales. Her husband would keep the kids for three hours so she could do something she loved. That was her time each week to really keep a part of her that was *her* and know that somebody else was taking care of the babies.

Think about how you're using your time, what you love to do, and how you can do more of what you love to do so that you can be happy and fulfilled. The baby/toddler stage is about going from organizing yourself to organizing yourself and other people. Organizing schedules, baby bags, childcare, and your child's memories.

You're creating new traditions and establishing your home. "Where do we want to go to church? How do we want to celebrate the holidays? What are our traditions for our family going to be?" There's a lot of work and planning that goes into that.

You're learning to let go of yourself and to embrace the whole idea of being a family beyond you and your husband. You gain new friendships and play groups of people who have kids about the same age. The friends that I made when my kids were babies are some of my best friends today, because we went through that experience together.

You're also establishing your mommy gut. You are your child's parent for a reason. They need you. You need them, and you know what's best for them. Better than any school, any doctor, your parents, your siblings, and your friends. You will gain a gut instinct about what is right for your kids, and that takes a long time to develop. At least it did for me.

The baby and toddler stages give you lots of organizational practice. Every two to three months, your kid is eating completely different foods, playing with completely different toys, and gaining new abilities. You have to organize their shots, their medicines, and their checkups.

Now that my kids are fifteen and sixteen, it does seem like those years were short, but I remember how long they were. And, no, I'm not to the point yet where I would really like to have the toddler years back. I would take a cuddly baby and a bottle of milk any day, but those toddler years were really, really a struggle for me.

Along with the nanny and the assistant, the Sunday Basket was my saving grace. Let me show you how it works.

THE SUNDAY BASKET

The Sunday Basket was the system I created to help me get on top of all the paper and daily "to dos" I had as an adult.

Everything starts with the Sunday Basket. I didn't realize it when I started the system years ago, but pretty much everything I know about organizing can be learned with the Sunday Basket. You will learn prioritization, as well as how to deal with mail, projects, and reference items.

It's a big deal to make a Sunday Basket. It usually takes ten hours to get everything together and done the first time. After that, the Sunday Basket becomes a tool that you will use week after week. It usually takes people about six weeks to get into the flow of using a Sunday Basket.

Some of you may be thinking, "Ugh, a basket, I don't even like baskets. That's so 1980s!" So before I go any further, I'll admit that yes, I'm a country 1980s kind of girl. But your Sunday Basket could be a box or a bag; I don't care. Just get some kind of container that you're going to use to collect all of the mail and papers that come into your life.

You will check this container on a regular basis. I check mine on Sunday—that's why I call it the Sunday Basket. It may be a Friday box for you, or a Tuesday bag, or whatever you want it to be, but it has to have a day and it has to be a container for paper.

Step 1 — Find all of your paper.

And I mean all of your paper. Your first basket is going to be one or two laundry baskets.

Grab a laundry basket and go on a scavenger hunt all around the house. You're going to pick up all of that paper that needs to be processed, like the mail you left in the car or the stuff you left in the garage on the way into the house. You'll search your laundry room, the counter by the bathtub, that space near your dresser. You'll look in the kitchen and on the dining room table.

Maybe you put something down when you went into the kids' room to tuck them into bed. You'll probably find paper everywhere: mail, catalogs, bills, forms to fill out, things that need to be filed, things that need to be shredded, all of it.

I don't want you to do anything with your paper. You're not processing it or taking any action whatsoever. You're just containerizing it all into laundry baskets.

If you fill two laundry baskets and there is still more paper in your house that needs to be processed, I want you to stop and do this process with two laundry baskets full of paper. Then start over again. Some people have lived in their houses for decades, and honestly, they could easily fill ten to twelve laundry baskets. I am not making any judgments. This is just a process of how to tackle it.

You may be thinking, "I need an accountant and a bulldozer. That's what I need."

No, you don't. You can do this. Just fill one laundry basket at a time. Do this entire system, adding another laundry basket and another. You didn't get into this situation overnight, and you're not going to get out of it overnight. We just have to start somewhere, or we're always going to be living in the piles of paper.

On average, people fill two laundry baskets.

You might think, "She's crazy, I won't even have one laundry basket full of paper." But when you really start picking up all the magazines, catalogs, newspapers, and kids' school papers, you'll have two laundry baskets. Then you'll be thinking, "Oh my gosh, two laundry baskets. I cannot believe I have two laundry baskets' worth of papers that need to be processed."

Finding your paper does two things. First, it gets the paper out of all the other rooms of your house. Now, everywhere you go, you're not going to see paper. That will bring down your stress level and give you some breathing space.

Second, when put all your paper in those laundry baskets, you will know where to look for things. When you find out that you were supposed to send in a permission slip, that's okay. It's somewhere in those two laundry baskets. It may take you fifteen minutes to find it, but it's not going to take you an hour and a half.

When you don't have a Sunday Basket, you have to look in your car, in the garage, and in every single room in your house to find that piece of paper. The beauty of the Sunday Basket is that all your paper is in one place, and all you have to do is start going through that basket.

Step 2 – Separate the active paper from the archive papers.

Make yourself a nice cup of coffee, or a glass of wine. Turn on mindless TV in the background, if that's what you like, or some nice upbeat music that's going to keep you energized. Sit down with your laundry basket.

Breathe.

Get another empty laundry basket and a trash can (or recycling bin). As you pull each piece of paper out of the laundry basket, you are going to divide them into piles.

1. If it's trash, just trash it.
2. Paper like insurance statements, tax returns, or the kids' report cards—anything you want to keep and file—goes in a to-file pile. They're a

long-term item you want to keep, but they don't require any action.

We are not going to file those now. Make a big pile of everything that needs to be filed, and then take that pile to wherever the filing cabinet is and put it there.

3. Make a pile of anything that needs to be shredded.

These three steps are going to get rid of anywhere from 60–80 percent of your papers in that laundry basket.

The only items left in your laundry basket are active papers . . . like the invitation to that graduation party you need to reply to and buy a gift for, the permission slips that need to go back to school, the bills that need to be paid, the email you printed out about the dates for the kids' summer camp that you need to add to the Google calendar, the Post-it note that's in there to remind you to buy a Father's Day gift for your dad. All of those things are what you now have left in the Sunday Basket. They are all actionable items.

Step 3 – Work on the actionable items in your basket.

Items that we need to make decisions on or do something with. This is what your Sunday Basket is all about.

The Sunday Basket only works if you set aside time in your calendar to do the Sunday Basket activities weekly. I'll be honest, some weeks that's two hours. Other weeks, I can get the Sunday Basket done in fifteen minutes.

Fifteen minutes, two hours, it doesn't matter. You need some time to go through this basket every week.

The first thing you're going to do is to take every single thing out of the basket and put those papers in a pile on the floor. Your basket should be empty.

Pick up every single piece of paper and say to yourself, "Can this wait until next Sunday?" If you're just starting out, or you're in a really busy phase of life, you're going to want to defer as many decisions as you can and put the papers back in the Sunday Basket.

There are two reasons for this. First, you do not want a lot on your to-do list, and second, the more you defer things week after week, the more often you actually decide not to do them at all. Fifty percent of your actionable Sunday Basket items never get done, and you will decide to recycle or shred them.

For example, we have Time Warner Cable. I needed to get digital adapter boxes for each of my TVs in order for them to receive digital cable a year from now. I kept putting that letter back in my Sunday Basket for probably two months before I finally called them and had the digital adapters sent to me.

When the digital adapters arrived, I took the actual boxes that were sent to me and I put those in my Sunday Basket. Then, I kept deferring the task of setting them up for about a month.

So, in addition to paper, you may have physical items in your Sunday Basket.

Any household projects that need to be done are going to end up in your Sunday Basket. And what a great place for them, right? Every week you get to decide: Is this the week I'm going to plant the vegetable garden? Is this the week we're going to call the guy to paint the house or to get new gutters? If the actual project does not fit in the Sunday Basket, put a note in the Sunday Basket to remind you.

As you go through the Sunday Basket process you will start to think, "Okay, nope. I'm not doing the Time Warner Cable project. Yes, I need to pay this bill. No, I don't need to pay that bill. Yes, we need to fill out this form. No, we don't need to fill out that form."

At the end of each session, you will have things in your Sunday Basket that will sit there until next Sunday for you. And you'll have a handful of things that are sitting in your lap or on the kitchen counter, things that you need to act on and do, either today or sometime this week.

Step 4 — Group like items together.

I particularly like slash pocket folders for this. Slash pocket folders are three-hole-punched plastic folders that are sold in the binder supply section of the store. Sometimes they have tabs on them, sometimes they don't. You can get them in clear, but usually you'll find them in assorted colors.

Slash pocket folders are how I organize the papers in my Sunday Basket.

After you have used your Sunday Basket for about four to six weeks, you're going to start thinking, "Oh my gosh. I know that I have to plan the VBS camp in August, but it is May, and every single Sunday, I'm going through and I'm touching eighteen different pieces of paper because I'm coordinating Vacation Bible School. Touching each of these pieces is driving me crazy."

Or, "We are going to go on vacation to Florida, and I have twelve pieces of paper that go with that." Or, "The kids don't go back to school until September first, but I'm collecting all these papers I need to keep track of until August first."

These are natural groupings of paper. What you need is a VBS folder, a first-day-at-school folder, and a going-to-Florida-vacation folder.

You don't want to start with slash pocket folders. Your paper, not your goals, will determine what your folders should be. If you do it the other way around, then you'll start thinking, "What would be the ideal folders?" There are no ideal folders. It's not a filing system. It's just a nice way to keep papers, little notes, and projects together.

Once you have these like items grouped together, it becomes much quicker to go through the Sunday Basket because instead of having to look at all of the papers that go with your vacation, you just need to look at the folder that says "Florida Vacation" and ask yourself, "Can this wait until next Sunday?" You might say, "Yeah, we're not leaving yet. I'll just add in all these little notes, or I'll rewrite my list, put it in there, and then put it back in the Sunday Basket. I don't need that folder out." Maybe the next folder is "Summer Tutoring." You might think, "Yeah, we need to keep that one out. I need to schedule that and talk to the teachers."

Creating your Sunday Basket is Organization 101

Before you jump into the One Hundred Day Home Organization Challenge, organizing ALL your papers, or working on your productivity, I want you to have a Sunday Basket. When you start organizing, it always gets more chaotic before it gets organized, right?

How many times have you started an organization project and had someone walk in and say, "You're organizing it? It looks like you're blowing it up."

Or sometimes you have to leave to take the kids to a doctor in the middle of that organizational blowup, and you don't even get back to it for three or four days. Then you're living in even *more* chaos before you can get organized, right?

There are a couple of things that you need to do to set yourself up for success before you try to organize your whole house. Start with a Sunday Basket. Then it doesn't matter if you're in the middle of organizing your closet and there are clothes everywhere and you can barely even walk through your bedroom. If your kid comes in and says, "Mrs. So-and-so needs that paper back," you can go straight downstairs, find the Sunday Basket, find that piece of paper, sign it, and give it to the kid. It takes maybe fifteen minutes.

If you don't have a Sunday Basket, this is what happens. You say, "Oh my gosh. I can't believe I took time for myself to organize my closet. I'm not being a good mother. I don't even know where these papers are—who am I to think I can get organized? This is insane. I need to just stop. I don't even know if I can do this."

I know because this is what I would think.

But if you can stop, go find that paper, and get back to what you're doing, you think, "This is great. I know where the important papers are, and I know where the bills are. I'm going to handle that every Sunday. It's okay for me to prioritize organizing my closet. I may not be organized yet, but I'm on my way, and I know where all the important papers are for our family while I do this for me."

Then, yes, it's okay. Let the laundry and the dishes pile up. Your house will not implode if you take two or three days to organize your master closet or if you take a couple hours a day to do the One Hundred Day Challenge so that your house functions better. You need to have one place—only one place—where all of those kinds of papers go, and then one time a week when you check it so you can stay on top of those requests and be the awesome, organized woman that you are.

You can download the Sunday Basket Quick Guide, SHRED Printable, and How to Sort Paper Printables at www.organize365.com/book-bonus.

Before we leave the accumulation years, it's time to look at all your childhood possessions you are still saving for yourself.

SAVING YOUR MEMORABILIA

What are you saving for yourself that you could get rid of?

I'm just going to be completely honest with you. I was supposed to write this chapter at least five other times, but every time, I found something different to do other than write it.

One day, I spent the entire day cleaning my house and doing all of the laundry. I procrastinated like I never procrastinate. I'm pretty good, even if there's something that's challenging. I might procrastinate the first time I do it, but the second time, I just buckle down and get it done. And this chapter has been procrastinated to the point that I cannot procrastinate anymore.

Okay, here's the deal. I redecorate my kids' rooms every three years with completely new paint, sometimes furniture, whatever. They get a whole new bedroom every three years because I think it is so fun. I look at their bedrooms like they are their apartments. For the most part, all of their stuff fits in their bedrooms.

I would classify my husband as a minimalist. He fishes and he golfs, but he has one fishing box and one golf bag. He has a few additional golf bags and a tackle box from family members who have passed away. He just doesn't have a lot of stuff. And he doesn't really want more stuff. That's just how he is.

That leaves me the entire house. The entire house is my domain. Maybe you are like me. I walked around the house this morning. I have dishes that have been out on the counter that I haven't washed for twenty-four hours. In the laundry room, I've completed all the laundry, but there is a whole bunch of stuff that I never finished folding or putting away.

On the bathroom counter, I have some Epsom salts my husband bought for me. I put one bag in the container we have. The other bag I never put away. The bed is not made. There are piles all over on my desk. Downstairs on the dining room table is a new wreath that I am making for the front door. As you go in the basement, there are piles of things in various stages that I am selling on Etsy.

In the storage room, I moved everything out of the way for the new air conditioning and heating systems, but there is a whole bunch of stuff in there that I never put back. So basically, any room that you walk into in this house, there is some task there that I haven't finished, right?

And yet, I will nag my daughter and not let her go to the movies until she puts away the makeup in our community bathroom. Not only that, I will think about it all day: "Well, she doesn't put away the makeup, so we need to have a reward and a discipline system for the makeup. You know what, maybe she just needs to do her makeup in her bedroom. But she says she doesn't have good lighting, so I'll hire an electrician to come in and put in track lighting in her room. And then I will buy these special lightbulbs I know about that are actually supposed to be the same spectrum as the sun. And then she will be able to do her makeup in her room, and then it will be out of the main living space, and everything will stay neat and organized because her makeup will now be in her bedroom."

Meanwhile, that doesn't change the fact that I never really finished the laundry, I haven't done the dishes, and all those other things I said. But because I know when I am going to get to those projects, or I'm busy (I'm working, for crying out loud. I'm not just playing on my phone all day or taking allowance money from my parents to go to the movies), it's okay if I make the messes because it's my house.

I am telling you this because, number one, I just think it is so true. I think this is how other mothers think. I look around and I see two pairs of shoes and a pair of socks in the living room, and I am ready to bite my daughter's head off. It is so easy to look around this house and harp on the things that I want Greg or the kids to get rid of, but everything in this house that is mine, well, why would I get rid of that? It's my house. It's my stuff. It's displayed where I want it. It's stored how I want it. Why would I get rid of it?

But what if something happens to me tomorrow and I'm gone, leaving my husband and my kids to deal with everything that is in, legitimately, my house? Because 85 percent of what's in this house is mine. It came from my childhood, or I bought it, or I brought it in here, or I created it.

Now you're probably not going to die tomorrow, but what I've noticed in compiling this list of ten things that I am going to get rid of is that a lot of these things have meaning, but the thing no longer holds the meaning.

I am holding on to a lot of items that hold memories, but not physical value. The more we can let go of our own possessions, the lighter our houses will feel and the freer we will be to move into our new passions.

Nine Items I Am Decluttering

#1 Old Decorations

The first thing that I am going to get rid of is fake trees. Carol, who organizes with me, is going to applaud like crazy. When she met me four years ago and she wandered through my house, I had a fake tree in every single room of my house.

You know, those fake trees that are in those little wicker basket pots. I had three big ones and two small ones and then a bush. Subtly trying to bring me into the new millennium, she said, "What are these?"

To which I replied, "Well, they are fake trees. You have to have a fake tree in every room of the house." Carol learned quickly that subtlety doesn't really work with me.

I took those fake trees from my parents' house. They had bought them probably in the early eighties when people actually did decorate with fake trees. I got them when they upgraded their decorating to what was probably current in the nineties. I was so excited to take all the fake trees.

I went to Kirkland's and Pier 1 recently. As I was walking around Pier 1, I realized they don't even sell fake trees anymore. They have these big, huge, awesome vases and all these different kinds of stems. That's when I realized, I have not been in a home décor store in six or seven years. I have not walked around Pier 1 or Kirkland's or Home Goods, any of those stores, in all that time.

I've been in survival mode, so busy taking care of my kids, parents, and jobs that I don't shop anymore. Like, ever. I never go shopping. And if I do, it's with a list, and I am in and out of there as fast as humanly possible. I am not shopping for décor or anything that I don't absolutely need.

I just wondered around Pier 1 for thirty minutes. It was so fun. I thought, "Oh my gosh. I like that little peacock," and, "Isn't that such a cool couch?" and, "I love elephants and giraffes. I should have elephants and giraffes in my house." I really looked around the house and realized it has been twenty years since I decorated this house.

#2 College Projects

So many of us hold on to our college textbooks and projects. I graduated with two majors and a minor. I was certified to teach kids from birth through eighth grade. I also had all the requirements to own and operate a daycare center. My goal when I graduated was to own a corporate daycare center.

For my senior project, I created a daycare center start-up plan. I picked out every single toy, every piece of furniture, and selected the curriculum for every room. I created the budget and everything.

My grandfather, who passed away last year at the age of 102, was 80 when I graduated from college. He was an engineer and made architectural drawings of this corporate daycare center for my graduation gift.

So many times, I have thought, "I need to declutter this. I really don't need this anymore."

But I love that I put so much time into that project, and the fact that I was able to figure out all the different pieces and parts to start a business when I was twenty-two. Then my grandfather made that into legitimate drawings, like we could go and actually build it. I love that! As a business owner, I just love that my entrepreneurial spirit goes that far back, and that somebody believed in me enough to make the drawings.

I have told that story probably twenty times. But you know what I have never done once? Shown anybody the blueprints. And the only time I have ever looked at the blueprints was when he gave them to me twenty-three years ago.

I was going to declutter both the blueprints and the binder, but once I looked at the blueprints again, I just couldn't. I did pitch the binder. My plan is to frame the blueprints and put them in my office.

#3 Books

Over the last three years, I have gotten rid of 80 percent of my books. I am peeling the onion back slowly over time on this one.

It is getting easier for me to get rid of books. My kids are fifteen and sixteen now, and a lot of my books were parenting books or books that I read while they were young children. Something clicked last year and I said, "I am never going to go back to those books again. My kids are really young adults now."

Along those lines, I realized that I have bookshelves in every single room of my house. I have a bookshelf in my bedroom. I have three in the loft. I have two in the living room. I have two in the family room. I have a bookshelf in our guest room. I have two in the basement family room. I have one in our storage room. And then, I have a whole closet full of bookshelves in the basement that holds all of my business supplies. For crying out loud, I also need to get rid of bookshelves when I get rid of books!

Finally this year, I was able to reduce and relocate ALL of our books to the three bookshelves in the loft. While it was difficult to let go of those books one at a time, I am so happy to have a small, well-maintained library in one location.

#4 Encyclopedias

When I was in eighth grade and my grandfather died, he had a set of 1964 encyclopedias in his house, and somehow, my family got them. I was so excited. It was 1985 and I had 1964 encyclopedias, which I loved. I would read the encyclopedias. I thought it was so cool. I wished we had current encyclopedias, but really, what I know now is that historical information in encyclopedias doesn't change that much. I was mostly reading about history anyway.

I think my parents finally decluttered the white set of 1964 encyclopedias when I was in college. As luck would have it, the encyclopedia door-to-door salesman came to our house when Joey was six months old.

Seriously. Door-to-door encyclopedia salesmen do still exist.

He did the whole spiel about how you need to have these encyclopedias for your kids, along with a few other educational book sets. It was something like $1,600. It was ridiculous.

But I was going to be the best mother and possibly home school. I was an educator, and my child was going to be so smart, blah, blah, blah. We bought it. They are beautiful.

The kids have used them a little bit over the years, but only when I've said, "Let's go look that up in the encyclopedia and send it into school."

Here's the thing. Nobody is reading the encyclopedias. I am not reading the encyclopedias. My kids look up everything on their iPad. The encyclopedias are big and bulky and they need to go. It was super hard to donate that big financial investment and childhood wish.

Ironically, it is also super hard to find people to take encyclopedias, even when you're giving them away for free. Very few people want them.

#5 Storage Containers

When I was in the accumulation phase of life with young kids, I needed a ton of storage containers. Every three months, I would go through the kids' toys, and their interests and developmental levels would be totally different. So I would need different sizes of storage containers for their toys.

Or, goodness gracious, Abby is like her own little pet store. She always has some different pet. Currently, we have two gerbils, a dog, a guinea pig, and now she wants hermit crabs. She always needs storage containers for all the food and hay and bedding that all of those creatures need. However, she is really the only person who is going down to the basement to get storage containers anymore.

I am continually using up the supplies we have and only buying what I need. I don't buy in bulk anymore. I also don't buy everything I could possibly want when I start a new hobby. In the past, I would think, "Okay, I am going to start scrapbooking. Let's create a whole scrapbooking room. Let's fill it with scrapbooking paper."

I'm not shopping like that anymore. When I do work on a scrapbooking project for a client, I go out and I buy what I need for that project. There might be some materials left over at the end, but I am not creating a whole craft room. So I don't really need storage containers anymore.

#6 Old Sporting Equipment

This is so funny. Hopefully, you can laugh along with me on this one. Okay, I was probably in eighth grade when my mom took us skiing for the first time. We lived in Akron, Ohio, and we went to Boston Mills to go skiing. We rented skis and skied up the slope on a tow rope and coasted down the little tiny bunny hill. We did this—quite happily—for three hours.

It was forty-five degrees and rained the entire time. We had to wear trash bags over our clothes as we skied. We looked like little California raisins coming down the hill.

My mom said, "Well, if the kids will ski for three hours in cold rain, they're skiers." She bought us ski boots, skis, the whole nine yards. We were in ski club and we skied for years. Once, when we were in high school, we even went to Colorado.

When Greg and I met, we went on ski trips every year for a couple of years. And after we got married, I think we skied once or twice and then stopped.

A few years ago, the kids started skiing with their school, and I was a parent chaperone who skied on the slopes. Those boots and skis that my mom bought for me twenty-six years ago are the same boots and skis that I skied on with my son. Now that he is sixteen, he does not need a chaperone if he goes skiing, and our daughter does not like to ski.

A couple of years ago, when I was still the skiing chaperone, I was maybe forty years old, still on my twenty-six-year-old skis, and I thought, "You know, when I've been skiing, I'm really sore the next day."

As I was going down the hill, I almost fell. And I decided, "You know what, I am done with it. I'm over it. I really don't want to fall skiing and break my leg and be out of commission for six months. I think I am done skiing." But of course, I put the skis and the boots right back in the basement, right where they were before.

My husband got rid of his skis and boots about five years ago. Here's the thing. It is time to get rid of the skis and boots. If we do go on a skiing trip with our kids, it's not going to be in Cincinnati. It's going to be in Colorado or somewhere that has something bigger than a hill to ski on, number one.

Number two, everyone else in my family is going to have to rent boots and skis. So am I going to save us seventy dollars by carting my own skis and boots while everybody else rents theirs? That's ridiculous.

And number three, I am pretty sure that they make boots and skis differently now than they did thirty years ago. And maybe I would feel better at the end of the day if I was skiing with more current equipment. So, all that to say, I am getting rid of my skis and boots.

#7 Old Stereo Systems

When I was in high school . . .

Again, notice everything I've mentioned is thirty years old. This is exactly what I am talking about. These are the things that you and I need to be looking at in our houses. Nobody is going to tell us it is time to get rid of the fake trees, encyclopedias, and the skis. That's all in our domain. We are going to have to hold ourselves accountable. Walk around the house and say, "Seriously, you don't need it. You are not using it. Eventually, someone else is going to have to take this out of your house. Let's decide."

So let's talk about the expensive stereo system. I babysat for kids all throughout high school and college. I spent my money on fast food and electronics. In 1988, I was obsessed with a store called Audio Craft. In the movie *National Lampoon's Christmas Vacation*, Clark Griswold (Chevy Chase) has a rich neighbor with a laser stereo system. When Clark falls from the roof, a missile of ice shoots out of his gutter and breaks the stereo. That exact model of stereo system was sold at this store. I drooled over it weekly.

I saved up all my babysitting money, and I bought a two-thousand-dollar Yamaha stereo system in 1988. It wasn't the laser system, but it had a five-disc CD player that was brand new to the market. It also had a tape-to-tape player, so I could make mix tapes from the radio.

Well, about ten years ago, I put the tape-to-tape component in the basement. Because who knows, it is part of the system. I might need it. I only use the five-disc CD spinner at Christmas.

The last two Christmases, every single CD that I put in the CD player skipped. This Christmas, I realized, "You know what, I don't think those CDs are skipping. I think the CD player doesn't work anymore." And this is a big— not gigantic, but it is big—old stereo system.

I cannot even tell you how many basements we have organized where we are carrying out big old stereo systems that people put in the basement because they didn't really work anymore, or because the people got a new one and they just put the old one in the basement. I understand; I almost did it myself! It's time to get rid of the whole stereo system.

I have a small stereo that has great sound that will play just one CD at a time. I can use that while we decide what we are going to do going forward. Two thousand dollars divided by twenty-eight years of use . . . do the math, and it comes to seventy-one dollars per year. Yep, it's okay to let it go.

#8 Old Framed Pictures

After we stop displaying custom-framed collages or artwork in my house, they go in the basement. They don't match the décor anymore. They are not going to match future décor. But I can't get rid of them. I don't know why. I know I'm not alone. Picture frames are a big category in our storage room organization jobs.

One quick tip: When you are putting smaller frames in storage with snapshots in them, decide if you want the picture, the frame, or both. When we organize storage rooms, we can easily empty out old picture frames and keep the pictures while donating the frames. This saves a ton of space.

I want to share with you how my larger art ends up in storage. Twelve years ago, I had the babies with me, and I was shopping with a friend. We were at Old Time Pottery and I found these two pictures for thirty-five dollars each that would work as art in my master bedroom. It was in my budget and I had no artwork in our bedroom, so I bought them.

They are two pictures of palm trees. I never loved them, but they totally matched the room. My husband is from Florida. We like to go to Palm Springs. I thought it would be fine. They have now been in my bedroom for twelve years. I don't really like them. They work, but I don't love them.

When I redo the artwork in this room with something that I love, something that I have taken the time to pick out, and not just to have something to go on the wall, these don't have to go in the basement. They can go to a resale shop. Or I can give them away. My goal is that at the end of eighteen months, my house will be completely decorated and I won't have any picture frames in my basement.

#9 Old Workout Equipment

There is something I have been asking my husband

to get rid of for the whole twenty years that we have lived in this house: his weight bench and weights. My husband was once a wrestler and cross country runner. He would lift weights with a friend at a gym.

He owned a weight bench and weights, which I am pretty sure he used in high school and college in his parents' basement. But they had moved to his condo. He didn't use them in the condo. They were in storage. And then after we got married, they moved here to our house, where he has not lifted a single weight.

Every time I've said, "Can we get rid of these?," it's, "Well, you know, I'm going to bulk up. I'm going to . . ." And then it was, "Well, we're going to have to do this with Joey, and this will be great." Joey is now sixteen and Greg is forty-nine.

Last night, we were in the basement looking at our brand new air conditioning and heater systems (which is what you do in your forties, you look at your brand new appliances), and I said, "You see these weights? Can I get rid of them now?" And he said, "Yeah, fine, get rid of them." I was like, "Yes!" I was so excited because I've wanted to get rid of those for such a long time.

A few days later, a friend took all the weights for her teenage boys. And you know what? A few weeks later the kids both asked me to get them workout equipment and weights. But here is the awesome thing. I did not want them to use those old cement-filled weights on a thirty-year-old bench. As luck would have it, a family member was getting rid of a Nordic Track weight system and a treadmill.

So now we will have a home gym area that our whole family can use, and I will feel safe having the teenagers use it. Just because you already own something doesn't mean it will be the best thing to use in the future when the need arises.

What About Your Stuff?

You can see that a couple of these things are going to take me twelve to eighteen months to get rid of. But as of today, I have decided they are going. Over the next eighteen months, all of these things will be leaving my house. And I think that is part of it. I always say the mindset is first and then the actions follow.

I hope I've given you some ideas of things that you can now go ahead and let go of, so that future generations don't have to decide what to do with your fake trees, college projects, and old sporting equipment. But you can still keep the memories of these things that you love and you saved for twenty, thirty years. It is the memories we have that we talk about with friends. We don't actually physically go get the encyclopedias when we tell people the encyclopedia story, right?

Back when I entered the accumulation phase of life, I expected it to be challenging, and it often was. But I was completely blindsided by the survival phase. The difficulties I'd encountered as a new mom and business owner were no match for the seven-year slide into the next phase of my life.

Phase Three

SURVIVAL

MY TRANSITION FROM ACCUMULATION TO SURVIVAL

I grew up with a very idyllic childhood. Literally, nothing bad ever happened to me. I used to joke that I lived in a bubble, and I liked it that way. I wanted to keep the bubble, and for a long time, I did just that.

Overwhelm

Around 2004, the bubble started to show some serious cracks. During the 2004-2005 school year, I went to 110 school and doctors' appointments for my children. None of these appointments were, "Oh, we just wanted you to come see the school play," or, "Oh, we're just going to have your child's regular checkup." Every single one of these 110 doctors' and school appointments were for more testing, trying out a new medication, analyzing results, setting up an education plan, fighting for this or that, or getting more funding.

It was all hard work, analytical stuff. I told myself it wasn't a big deal. After all, I was working from home, so I had the time to do it. We still had a great income, the kids were in a great school, and I was going to fight for these kids and get everything that they needed done.

I had been told as a kid, "You can do anything you put your mind to," and I believed it. I still believe it to this day. I can't do everything at the same time, I've learned, but I can do anything I put my mind to.

The summer of 2005, I lost it. I just freaked out on my husband, so much so that he had to take the kids away. I went up to my bedroom, and that's when I counted and realized I'd been to 110 school and doctors' visits.

I thought, "Well, no wonder I'm losing it. Who can go to meetings every third day where you're deciding your child's future and what they need? That is a lot to put on a person, right?"

My business was still going great financially, so there was no doctor too far, no school too expensive. We would just work harder.

At that time, one of the kids' doctors said, "You're under a lot of pressure."

She'd been talking about antidepressants, and I said, "All right, which kid are we going to start on that?"

They said, "No, it's you who needs to be on an antidepressant."

And I said, "Me? Depressed? No, I'm not depressed."

They said, "Well, you're under a lot of stress. It's very overwhelming."

And I thought, "All right, I'll try it." So I started Lexapro around Christmastime. We were going home, and I took one of the pills.

Wrong Medicine. Wrong Time.

When we showed up at my parents' house, I was walking, but I felt like I was floating above the room, looking down at myself saying, "Talk. You should talk, you're not talking."

My parents asked, "What's the matter with you?"

I said, "I'm fine." And I didn't talk the whole day.

Can you imagine? I talk all the time.

So I'm floating above myself, looking down, going, "Talk, talk," and I couldn't talk, so I never took that pill again. I thought, "Well, what's the point in having an antidepressant where I can't talk and I can't function? That's not a solution for me. So antidepressants are not for me, right?"

One year later, in January 2006, my parents separated. Now this shocked me, of course, but really it shocked the whole community. I mean, these were the high school sweethearts that no one ever thought would get separated or divorced. In school, we were called the "*Leave It to Beaver* family." June and Ward Cleaver were getting separated. My bubble burst that day, and things started getting harder.

Next, Creative Memories' leadership changed. In 2008, the company declared bankruptcy.

There were increasing demands on my time. The kids had more needs. Our financial needs were growing. My income was dropping. Our personal economy was collapsing about fourteen months before the collapse hit the whole country. Our children's medical needs consumed 50 percent of our take-home pay and would continue to do so for the next six years.

I picked up a couple of housecleaning jobs, which really helped. I was also in another direct sales business that was still generating an income. I worked part-time as a computer teacher at a private school two days a week. I tutored two students at my home after school.

I was also doing a bunch of these one-off jobs: organizing spaces, painting rooms in clients' houses, taking down wallpaper. Anything home-related that people didn't have time to do, I was doing.

On my tax return in 2008, I had nine Schedule Cs. Nine different bona fide businesses that I was running during that year to earn income for our family.

This started a pattern for me. From 2007 until 2012, I had a bazillion Schedule Cs on my tax return. I was working anywhere and doing anything that I could for work. Anything that I knew how to do proficiently, I was marketing as a service. I was over-accumulating jobs.

Welcome to the Sandwich Generation

Adding my parents' needs to my plate launched me into the sandwich generation. I was trying to make money, trying to meet my kids' needs, trying to help my parents, and trying to keep my household afloat.

Then in August 2008, my father was hospitalized. We thought he was going to die. He survived, but he got sicker over the next nine months before he finally passed away in May 2009.

Those nine months were a whirlwind. I would get a call and think, "Oh my gosh. You know, he might die today." I would jump in the car and drive the four hours to my dad's home, leaving my children to go take care of him.

Because my parents were divorced at this time, my sister and I had power of attorney. We had to make the financial and medical decisions. Whenever I was called home or I could go home, I did. I knew that those last few days with my father, every one that I could get with him, would be in my memory bank forever.

<u>Nothing was planned that year. Nothing.</u>

I was the only one who knew what medications my kids took and how to help them with their homework in the ways that worked best with their learning styles. I would just fly out of the house like a bat out of hell, and Greg would be stuck with these kids and this house that was starting to fall apart around us because we were just surviving. For seven years, we were in a state of survival.

After my father passed, my sister and I had to plan the funeral and settle the estate. And after the estate was settled, I tried to get our lives back in order.

I realized that my job situation wasn't really working. It wasn't predictable. I decided I would go back to full-time teaching; that would give us a consistent paycheck. That, plus my husband's paycheck, was not enough for our living expenses, but at least it would be consistent. And I could try to do something else, too.

Maybe we could make it work. The whole economy had collapsed. We weren't the only people struggling. I was just so grateful to have a job, to be employed, to be earning a wage.

I went back to work full-time in the fall of 2010. Well, by the spring of 2011, it was too much. Having the kids in two separate schools, working full-time, and creating individual lesson plans for my students kept me working until midnight and up at five.

Breaking Point

I had a couple of people who kept saying to me, "You know, you're depressed. You need to take care of it."

And I thought, "No, I'm not."

Then one day, I was driving on the highway. I can't remember where I was going, but I remember exactly where I was when I thought, "If I veer the car over and I hit that cement wall and I die, then I'll be out of this."

Then I thought, "Well, I can't do that, because Greg doesn't know the kids' medication dosages. He would know to call this one doctor, but I don't even think he knows that Abby's seeing a new doctor yet."

The educational and medical stuff with my kids changes so fast, I'm just in charge of it. And if anything happens to me, Greg will call the doctors and they'll explain what's going on. That's our plan.

So I thought, "Well, I can't do that, because I can't leave him."

So I kept driving. I thought, "Well, if I just keep driving all the way to Florida . . ." Then I thought, "No, that won't solve your problem. Now you're in Florida, the kids are at home, you're going to have to turn around and go back." So I thought, "If I got our whole family in the car . . ."

It hit me. "Oh my gosh, I'm depressed. Where are these thoughts coming from? I cannot believe I'm thinking these thoughts." I'd been so busy surviving and getting through and doing, I hadn't realized how bad things were getting.

I had been asking doctors for antidepressants for probably eighteen months prior to this. Every time I'd go in for a routine checkup, I'd ask, "Can I get an antidepressant?" And they'd say, "Hmm, no."

A day or two later, I was at the doctor's office with the nurse practitioner. So I said, "While we're in here, could we talk about antidepressants?"

She said, "Sure, to help you with your migraines?"

And I thought, *Shut up, Lisa.* "Yes, to help me with my migraines." *Let's go with that.* I just needed something. Whatever I had to say to get an antidepressant, to try it, to not want to drive my whole family into a cement wall, that's what I was going to do.

She said, "Oh sure, we'll start you on Cymbalta." I'd read that Cymbalta and Effexor are the two hardest antidepressants to get off of once you get on them, but at that point, I did not care. So I got the Cymbalta, brought it home, took it.

Now I didn't know it at the time, but not only was I depressed, I was also not so fun to live with. My way of trying to control the situation was to become very demanding with everyone, including the cat. I'd yell, "Get off the bed, why are you on the bed?"

I took the Cymbalta and by day three, I remember waking up at six in the morning to go to work and finding the cat in the bed. I pushed snooze on the alarm and started talking to the cat. "Good morning, Ozzy! Ozzy's so cute."

I was laughing and playing with the cat, and I thought, "Oh, I'm happy!" I don't think it was necessarily *happy*, but I wasn't yelling at anyone anymore. It was like I'd had a couple of glasses of wine all the time.

One time, after the Cymbalta really started kicking in, the kids were jumping on the couch and Greg said, "The kids are jumping on the couch."

I said, "I know, isn't that so cute? We should just let them be kids. Maybe we should video it."

He said, "No, no, it's not cute. We don't jump on the couch. Who are you? Discipline them."

I said, "Why? You know I'm always disciplining, maybe they just need more love, maybe I need to be more lenient, maybe I . . ."

He said, "Oh my gosh. I love that you're not yelling at me and bitching at me all the time, but could we have order, like, could you care?"

And I didn't care. That was the great thing about Cymbalta. I was no longer stressed. I was fine with the mess. I was fine with the kids. I really just didn't care.

Greg said, "You have to care," and I said, "Well, I don't care right now," and that was my coping mechanism.

It was okay for me to not care.

I'm just telling you, if I had kept caring as much as I had cared, our family might not be here today. So it was worth it for me to go on the medicine and have that whole summer of pretty much not caring.

"Oh yeah, well, it's a good thing we have credit," I always said. "It's a great thing we have credit, because we're using it. There are all these people with this depression we're having that can't get credit. But because we're old, we have credit. So we can use it." Which we did. We maxed out everything we had.

By the fall of 2011, I'd been on Cymbalta maybe four months, and I knew that I was done using it. It had done exactly what it needed to do. It gave me the break from caring so much about everything.

Before I went on the Cymbalta, I was picking all of the battles, all of the time. I had lost my ability to prioritize. I had lost my ability to see the big picture. I had lost my ability to see where we were going. I was so stuck in the day-to-day grind that I was barely surviving. I just couldn't get any perspective.

Being on the Cymbalta gave me perspective. It gave me the ability to pick my battles again, as well as the ability to make a game plan. I spent that summer surviving with the kids in a happier way and thinking, "Okay, I cannot fix everything I want to in the world, in my family, in my home, in our finances—so because I can't fix everything, what's the top thing I want to focus on for the kids' school? The top thing for the kids' medical? The top thing for our house? The top thing for my finances?" As opposed to trying to focus on twenty things under every single category.

It was frustrating for me to learn that I move faster than most of the people in my family. You're going to laugh and say, "Lisa, you move faster than most of the people in the world!" It's probably true; I just move really fast. I get a lot done.

I learned that I needed to pick something that we could work on: Abby and I, Joey and I, Greg and I, the house and I. And focus on just that one thing until mastery and then add one more.

Sometimes when I would add one more, the thing we had mastered would go away and I would realize, "Oh, I'm moving too fast, we need to just bask in the glow of the fact that we've mastered this one task for a little longer before I start on my goal of mastering another one."

There are things I learned in that time that made me who I am today, and I am very grateful for that. I'm a much more mellow person today than I was in the past. I don't think I can fix everything immediately like I used to think I could.

I think I can help.

I think I can move you forward.

I think I can stand alongside you.

But I don't think I know everything you're going through, or that I can fix all of your problems. And I think those are good things that came out of this experience.

In the fall of 2011, I realized that I had come out the other side. Financially, we were not where we needed to be, but mentally I had made the transition. And I'm telling you, mental happens before physical every single time. In this case, it happened about twenty-four months before the physical.

To save money, we had pulled Joey out of his private school and enrolled him in public school for the 2011-2012 school year. Within a few weeks, we knew he needed to transition back to his private school.

At the same time, I weaned myself off the Cymbalta. By November, I was completely off the meds, and I was back in the real world. In December, I quit my job. In February, we put Abby in the same private school that Joey was in. On January 1, 2012, I started the blog Organize 365. The start of my full-time professional organizing business followed in April.

I had increased our expenses and reduced our income hugely. And I had gone off my antidepressant. But at that point, I could handle it. From that point forward, I knew that I was ready. I had made the transition from Accumulation to Survival.

One out of every ten Americans is on an antidepressant. So if you are on one, you are not alone. I needed it, and I needed it for a short amount of time. I do not know if anybody else in my extended family has ever been on an antidepressant. My family genetics tend to be pretty positive; I don't know anyone in my family that has ever been depressed. In my case, it was situational.

I share this because I don't know if these stories are shared very much. My transition from childhood to the accumulation stage of life was a walk in the park. The seven-year transition from the accumulation stage to the survival stage just about did me in.

After I was off the Cymbalta, quit my job, and started Organize 365, I looked around my house and said, "Who made this big mess?" Everything was unorganized.

I came home from the grocery store. It was the first day the kids were at school, and I was back at home for the first time in over eighteen months. I walked in with bags from the grocery store and the counters were full, so I thought I would put stuff in the cabinets. I opened every single cabinet, and they were all full.

So I put the bags on the floor. Then I realized that not a single drawer, not one single cabinet, no countertop, *nothing* in my house was organized anymore. I had been surviving for so long that I didn't even recognize our house. My kids at that time were ten and eleven, and we still had sippy cups in the cabinets!

Life moved faster than I could keep up. And at one point it moved so fast, it was going to run me right over. So I had to use medication to slow it down enough that I could get back on and start running again.

I needed to unload some of my responsibilities. I started with anything I could outsource.

TEN HOUSEHOLD TASKS YOU CAN OUTSOURCE

I am a wife, a mother, and a business owner. Over the last twenty years, I have juggled those three commitments in various ways. And what I've come to understand is that no one person can do everything.

I have tried all of the ideas where you have your kids and your husband help you with the household tasks in order to free up some of your time. I do many of those, but what do you do when there's not enough of you and your children and your husband to get everything done?

In order to grow my business over the last twenty years, I have always hired help. Sometimes that is in the form of help to actually help my business—for instance, a personal assistant or an editor. But more and more, I find that the tasks I need to outsource most are household related.

For those of us in the survival phase of life, the sheer amount of hours spent in our car, or in service to our family and work, creates a vacuum of hours available to allocate to necessary home-based activities.

According to the Pew Research Center, 71 percent of females aged thirty-four to forty-nine are in the workforce[2].

For the vast majority of you, organization is a tool that allows you to do something else: grow your career, take care of your kids, strengthen your marriage, or pursue your hobbies. You're trying to get more organized so that you have more time to do the things that you love—and organizing is not one of them.

When I added up every task that my husband and I did that was household-related, I realized we were spending thirty-five hours a week cooking, cleaning, doing laundry, paying bills, grocery shopping, and the like.

The average household with children under eighteen requires twenty-eight hours of household-related tasks per week. Among married couples, men account for ten hours of tasks on average and women eighteen hours.[3]

---

[2] Pew Research Center tabulations of the 2014 March Current Population Survey from the Integrated Public Use Microdata Series (IPUMS), http://www.pewsocialtrends.org/2015/03/19/comparing-millennials-to-other-generations/#!19.

[3] Kim Parker and Wendy Wang, "Modern Parenthood: Roles of Moms and Dads Converge as They Balance Work and Family," *Pew Research Center* (blog), March 14, 2013, http://www.pewsocialtrends.org/2013/03/14/modern-parenthood-roles-of-moms-and-dads-converge-as-they-balance-work-and-family/.

Here are ten household tasks that you can outsource to free up your time for what is most important to you.

#1 Dry Cleaning and Laundry

Many people know that you can outsource dry-cleaning. You can even have someone come pick that up from your house. But did you know that you can also outsource your laundry?

I was listening to a podcast by a single male entrepreneur who didn't do his own laundry, and it just blew my mind. People don't do laundry? How do you get dressed? Do you just buy new clothes every day? I didn't know what you would do if you didn't do your own laundry.

I love to do our laundry. It really is a therapeutic chore for me, as crazy as that sounds. But adding up all the different times I walk into the laundry room, it takes three or more hours a week for me to do all of our laundry.

On a busy week, I took my laundry over to the Laundromat and had them do it for me. I did all of the towels and jeans at my house to save money. The Laundromat has a ten pound minimum, and I think I had twelve pounds. I got the premium service, so it was a $1.39 a pound instead of $1.20 a pound, which meant they hung everything up.

Now if you are depressed and you're looking for something that would be really fun, take ten pounds of laundry to a place that has a ten-pound minimum and pay the extra nineteen cents a pound to do the premium hang-up service. This is the best. They hung up every single one of my daughter's camis on a different hanger. They even hung up my bra like it was an actual bra on a little person on the hanger.

I've never had my laundry done so well, ever. It cost around eighteen dollars after tax, which is a lot of money to spend on laundry. But that week, I didn't have any time and I thought, "You know what? When I get super busy and I can't keep up, you bet I'm going to be dropping my laundry off. They do such a great job and eighteen dollars is worth it for what would have been two loads of time-consuming socks-and-underwear laundry."

#2 Housecleaning

This probably should have been number one. There have been various seasons over the years when I've had someone clean my house regularly, and it is so awesome. I am not a fastidious cleaner. I prefer things to be straightened and organized.

So having someone deep clean our house every other week is a luxury that our whole family enjoys. It allows me to not worry or stress out when messes happen in between cleanings.

#3 School Transportation

Both of my children attend private schools that are thirty minutes from our house (in opposite directions from one another!). For one of those schools, the parents were able to go in together and get a private bus chartered for the students. That saves me three or more hours of driving a day.

I've also run into the problem where both children need to be picked up at the same exact time. My solution was to hire a local high school student to pick up my daughter, get her a snack, take her to the library, get her homework done, and bring her home one hour later.

Not only did I solve my transportation problem, but my child had eaten a snack and had her homework done by the time I saw her. Worth every penny.

#4 Yard Work

There are a number of repetitive, yard-related tasks that a homeowner needs to accomplish. Just like hiring someone to clean your home, hiring out lawn maintenance can save a lot of time.

Three services that are pretty common are snow removal, yard fertilization, and grass cutting.

You may not need these services all the time, but if you're in a busy season in your business, or if your kids have been sick for a while and you're just drowning, you can hire someone to help get you caught up again.

#5 Shopping

I love to outsource my shopping to Amazon. As a matter of fact, my husband just took over doing all the bills recently, and he saw how much I love to outsource all of my shopping to Amazon.

When my kids walk into the room and say, "My headphones are broken," I just pull out my phone, order the headphones, and they're on their way. I don't even think about it because, for me, going to the store to get headphones is going to be forty minutes round trip, minimum. And the odds of me doing it within two days are very, very low. By the time I would actually get to the store, Amazon has already delivered the box.

#6 Projects

I LOVE to do projects. But as the demands on my time (especially driving time) have increased, I have less and less time to do household projects.

Sometimes there are projects that you want to get done for a holiday gift or a graduation, or there's an event that this project needs to be done for. Projects are something that can be easily outsourced.

There are people who will take all your kids' school shirts and turn them into a quilt. Or take all your photos and put them into photo albums. Or come in and organize your whole basement for you.

I love the feeling of checking a big project off my list, and I always wonder why I didn't outsource it sooner.

#7 Meals

You can outsource the whole meal-making process to a place like Dream Dinners or My Girlfriend's Kitchen. You can either make a bunch of meals all at once and freeze them (no meal planning, grocery shopping, or cleanup required) or pay extra to have the place actually make the meals for you. They will be bagged and ready to go right into your freezer.

You can also prepare frozen meals in bulk at home. I streamline our meals on one Sunday each month. I get everything I need, and I make ten freezer meals in a couple of hours and put them in our freezer. Then I pull them out as we need them throughout the month.

#8 Grocery Shopping

Every day, more grocery stores are adding an online shopping and pickup service at the store. I haven't tried it yet, but I'm excited to test this out soon with my hubby. I'm pretty sure he will still go inside to get deli meats, but other than that, it can all be done online.

Even if your grocery store is charging five dollars per pick up, this will save you an hour of parking, shopping, and checking out. Five dollars an hour seems like a great deal to me. My friends who have started doing this have noticed their grocery bills are much lower because they are not adding items to their carts as they shop.

This is an amazing gift for anyone who works full time or has little kiddos!

#9 Bookkeeping - Bill Paying - Paper Filing

Did you know you are your family's CEO? Well, you are. If you are short on time, you might just want to hire a bookkeeper for your family finances, bill payments, and monthly filing. Seems decadent, I know, but definitely a possibility.

Time is time, and you may want someone else to pay those bills so you can spend another hour a week playing with your kids or talking with your hubby.

I've seen this happen routinely with the elderly. They reach a point where they're not physically able to write checks anymore, or they have a hard time keeping up with all the varying bill due dates.

They have the money in the account, but just the thought of, "This is due on the tenth and that is due on the fourteenth" becomes very overwhelming. You can someone to open all their mail, write their checks, balance their checkbooks, get cash from the ATM, take them shopping, and bring them home.

#10 Scheduling, Phone Calls, and Errands

For all those miscellaneous tasks that eat up your time and energy, consider hiring a personal assistant.

Keep reading. It's not as scary or ostentatious as you think.

Have you ever wanted to clone yourself? I think you know where I'm going here. The role of homeowner today is not the same as it was even ten years ago. We need out-of-the-box thinking to arrange our days so that they meet our needs. We need to make sure we are not just cramming everything that "needs" to get done into the day until we collapse into a coma at night.

I have to admit, the first time I really suggested this to someone and even thought about it for myself, I thought, "Well, la-di-da that you need to have a personal assistant," but it's so true. With so many of the people that I've organized for in the last twelve months, I would look at them when we got done organizing and say, "You need a personal assistant."

Hiring a personal assistant, depending on where you are in your career, is a very logical thing to do. I have a part-time professional administrative assistant, and it's awesome. All those things that I'd never gotten around to in my business that needed to be done are finally getting done.

For me, hiring an assistant is an investment in my business so I can work four days a week and not five. I had been working five or six days a week for years, and I realized that was putting way too much pressure on me and on our family. I was constantly complaining that I didn't have enough time to work.

Recently, when Joey was sick, it was no big deal that I took the day off. And the following week when Greg was home on Friday, it was no big deal for me to take that day off, too. I can usually find four days a week when I can really put the pedal to the metal and focus on my business. I don't have to sacrifice my business goals for the sake of my family—and vice versa—because I'm using an assistant to do the repetitive tasks that would eat up the limited hours I have available to work.

I've helped my corporate clients to do the same. Even with all the technology available to us today, busy, productive women often need help with the routine tasks both in business and at home. Last year, I helped two corporate executives streamline their home organization and their jobs for maximum productivity. In both cases, the corporations hired personnel to support the executives once we created a plan for how this additional staff would help increase productivity and revenue.

Why I Outsource So Many Household Tasks

We underestimate the number of things that are on our plates.

Forty years ago, being a wife and a mother and taking care of your home was a full-time job. Today, you're a wife, a mother, you take care of your home, and you usually have a full-time job.

Forty years ago, kids went to a school that they could walk to down the street. Their mothers weren't spending twenty hours a week driving, like we are. Really look at your time.

I have a part-time driving job. I have a full-time housekeeping job. I have a regular job. I'm a mother. I have all of these roles. I have too many roles! When you get to the point that you have all these roles that you love, it's just not physically possible to manage. Something is going to suffer or you're going to outsource some of it.

So I outsourced dry cleaning, but not laundry. I outsourced fertilizing, but not grass cutting. I outsourced two days of driving my daughter, but not the other days. I outsourced some of our shopping, but not our grocery shopping. See how I made choices?

That way, I did the majority of the school driving, but not all of it. I did the majority of the laundry, but not all of it. I did the majority of the shopping, but I didn't physically do all of it. I was able to get everything done to the level I wanted, and I'd still have enough time to go for a walk with Greg every night after work and to read a book for a couple hours on a Sunday afternoon.

I want to make sure our marriage is the best it can possibly be, because my number one goal is to stay married for the rest of my life. That's my number one goal before anything else ever gets done, and that was the area I was always cutting short.

Whenever the kids needed me, work needed me, or the house needed me, I would cut out the time that I spent with Greg. Once I realized that, what I did instead was I hired out as much as I could, and I increased the amount of time I spent with Greg. We probably spend two to three hours a day together now, when it used to be twenty minutes a day. That was a conscious decision I had to make.

So yes, I pay for a whole bunch of things that you probably don't pay for, but I do that so I can just sit on the back patio with my husband for an hour every day and talk to him after work. We also watch an hour's worth of TV every night. You probably wouldn't have guessed I watch that much TV, would you?

Right now we're watching the series *24*. Let me just tell you, it's like crack. Don't start it if you don't have Netflix, because oh my gosh. We'll watch two or three episodes a night. One day we watched six. Yes, six episodes of TV! That's a ridiculous amount, but we love it, and it's great for our relationship.

I hope that this has inspired you and given you a few new ideas. Like I said, maybe you'll never do any of these things. But if your whole family gets the flu for a month and you're drowning, I want you to have resources to survive. Take all your laundry and have them do it at the Laundromat. That'll be the best hundred dollars you ever spent. Or go hire some high school kid to pick up your kids every day after school for a week, while you immerse yourself and organize your house.

This won't happen overnight, but you can slowly start replacing one disliked or time-consuming task with a high-value time investment. Over the past twenty years, I have diligently made these choices, and I've not been afraid to outsource many tasks, both business and home-related, to others. It is a big part of why I am so productive and so happy with my life.

Cha-Ching

Yep, I know most of these ideas cost money. You'll need to make some choices. Do you have more time or more money? If you answer, "Neither," then you just have to say to yourself that not everything is going to get done. You have to choose.

It's okay. You might not treat your yard or do any household projects. I have been there. But 70% of us are working. What is your time worth? If you are earning twenty-five dollars an hour at your job, can you outsource three hours of household tasks to a teenager for twenty-five dollars and save yourself two hours?

What do you LIKE to do? For years, a friend and I traded laundry for meals. I like doing laundry and she likes to cook. I did her kids' laundry (three to five loads) and she made two dinners a week for me. We didn't outsource the work, but we each did what we liked, and we got the work done quicker.

Ready for a lightbulb moment? Why not take your favorite item on this list and offer to do that task for a few friends? They can either pay you or you can trade out a few tasks you don't want to do as much.

There is always a way if you keep thinking and are open to out-of-the-box possibilities.

Once I had outsourced all I could, it was time to streamline the tasks I had left to consume as little time as possible.

Ten Things to Do on Sunday

If there is any way for me to get an extra two minutes of productivity in a day, I'm going to try to figure out how to do that. If you can get two minutes a day, that's fourteen minutes a week, which is an hour a month, which is twelve hours a year.

Two minutes a day makes a big difference in the grand scheme of things. I'm constantly looking at how I can be more productive, more efficient, and get the routine things in life done quicker so that I have more time to do the things I love to do—like podcasting and projects and going on walks with Greg and our dog, Hunter.

Pick Your Poison

How do you want to divide your twenty-eight to thirty-five hours of housework up during the week?

You can spend four to five hours on it every single day, seven days a week, or you can do six to eight hours on a Sunday and one to two hours each weekday, but either way, you'll need to put that time in just to keep your house maintained.

I'm talking about doing the laundry, cooking, grocery shopping, making sure the calendar is up to date, and paying the bills.

There are two ways people tend to approach things. They either do a little bit every day, or they do a whole lot in one day so they have a bunch of days that they can take off.

The easiest way to know which kind of person you are is to think about how you do laundry. If you prefer to start a load of laundry every day and have it clean, folded, and put away at the end of the night, you will probably prefer to do two to three hours' worth of housework every single day.

I am a get-all-the-laundry-done-in-one-day kind of gal. I like to take all day Sunday to do my household chores.

After church, Greg makes lunch for everyone, and I start the laundry. I do laundry all day. Usually, I actually start laundry on Saturday and run a couple of loads so that by Sunday, I'm folding a load, drying a load, and washing a load. At this point, we are outsourcing housecleaning, so I do not clean our house.

Then I do the dishes, plan the week, pay the bills, fill up all the pill dispensers, and refill any medicines that need to be refilled.

When using this method, it's best not to leave any tasks for Monday, because here is what happens: You leave a couple of things that you're going to do until

Monday or Tuesday, and then Monday at 4:⁚ something comes across your desk that has handled that day. You don't have the option of leaving at 5:00 p.m., so now you're leaving at 5:15 p.m. So you're fifteen minutes late, right?

Then on your way home, you find out that your mom needs you to come over and change a lightbulb. And I know that sounds ridiculous, but this is what happens in the sandwich season of life.

It takes an hour to get there and change the lightbulb, say hi, and come back. Even though she only lives two miles from your house, that's an hour. This is not out of the ordinary. These kinds of things happen to you all the time.

Now, you're an hour and fifteen minutes late getting home from work which means that your kids, if they're old enough, have fended for themselves. Whatever you were planning for dinner is no longer what you're having, or you've picked up fast food on the way home because you have to be at the Brownie meeting at 7:00 p.m. and there's not enough time to prepare whatever you were going to prepare and get to that meeting on time, right?

This can happen with any of a myriad of things. You find out that your kid has a fever, you have to go to school for an extra meeting, you get a flat tire, you don't feel like having chili that night. Lots of things happen that derail us once Monday morning starts.

When I look at productivity and what I get done, I always go back to this mantra: I can only control myself. I can't control my kids. I can't control my husband. I can't control my website crashing. I can't control the school schedule. There are so many things that are outside of my control.

The only thing that is inside of my control is how I organize my time and get things done in a timely manner so that I have more freedom and bandwidth to handle the unexpected things of life that always happen.

Yes, they do always happen. Unexpected things are guaranteed. It's not like if you get organized, you're no longer going to have to deal with unexpected events. You'll just be able to handle them better. I take Sundays for myself to not focus on work at all. Those are my days to think about what the house needs, what Greg needs, what the kids need, and what I need.

Here are ten things you can do each Sunday to have a more productive week.

#1 Plan your upcoming week on paper.

I love my Google Calendar, but when you physically write down your upcoming schedule, there is a connection between your brain and your hand that helps cement in your brain what your week is going to look like.

Writing out your schedule for the week will he figure out where you're going to fit in those extra tasks. Maybe you need time to work on a Bible study or you want to plan your next vacation. You could chunk that time in somewhere. This is also when I schedule in driving time to all our appointments.

There's a widely circulated maxim that for every hour you spend planning, you save three to four hours by avoiding the delays that come from redundancy, waiting for information, being unprepared, and poor task management.

Download my weekly planner printable worksheet at www.organize365.com/book-bonus.

#2 Put all items related to meetings, networking, school, and sports into the car on Sunday night.

When I make a pile on the kitchen counter of what I need for the next day, it is stressful, and I'm constantly reminding myself of things all morning. "Don't forget the mail," I think. "Don't forget the extra lunch box." If I put it in the car, it frees up my mind the next day to be thinking about other things like, "Don't forget to feed the kids this morning." There are only so many things that I can focus on each morning.

On Sunday night, if I know that I'm going to organize a kitchen on Thursday and I need to make sure I have lazy Susans in the back of the car, I don't wait until Wednesday night to put those in there. I do it Sunday night. I look at my entire week, and if there's anything that I can put in the car ahead of time, I do.

#3 Make a list of all the people you need to call this week, complete with phone numbers, and put it in your car.

After I drop my kids off at school, or when I get in the car on the way to go pick them up, I am in the car twenty-five or thirty minutes without kids. If I have the list of who I need to call this week, I can pull over, see who I need to call, call them, and get back on the road.

#4 Take care of all your food needs on Sunday.

If you go to the grocery store on the weekend, take an extra thirty minutes on Saturday or Sunday and bag up individual portions of everything for the upcoming week. That makes it really easy to pack a lunch. Just grab a bunch of different bags, make a sandwich, and put it in the lunch box.

#5 Open and process your mail once a week.

By Wednesday, I'm just surviving to get to Friday night. I will throw the mail unopened into the Sunday Basket. On Sunday, I will pull out all that mail and make sure to open and process everything.

#6 Get out cash.

I love this one.

Most people get paid on Friday. I look at our week ahead, determine how much cash we need, get it out on Friday night, and divide it up into envelopes. How often have you thought, "Shoot, I need to get another twenty bucks from the ATM." How long does that take you?

#7 Pick up the dry cleaning and do all the laundry.

I have talked to many working women who tell me all the time that they can't get to the dry cleaner, which means they can't get to the clothes they like to wear.

My kids go to a private school, and I buy enough uniforms for five days of the week so I can do my laundry on the weekend. (I also do a few loads on Wednesday night.)

#8 Pick up prescriptions and fill weekly medicine dispensers.

Every weekend, I fill up the weekly pill dispensers. Then, I put in an order to refill any prescriptions that are running low.

#9 Charge and reboot all of your electronics.

If I did not have this on the list, I don't think I would ever turn off my phone all the way. Do this once a week with your computer, and it will help clear out your cache and just make everything run better.

I charge everything, including backup cell phone batteries. I make sure my hot spot and Chromebook are charged. If you realize that you need one of your devices on Wednesday morning as you're running out the door for a meeting and it's not charged, then it does you no good.

#10 Do all the dishes, empty all the trash cans, and run the dishwasher.

I tend to run out of steam, and I don't want to do the dishes. I don't know why dishes is the thing I always put off doing. If you stop by my house, it's likely my dishes aren't done.

If I can do all the dishes, empty the kitchen trash, empty all the trash out of my bedroom and all the bathrooms, and run the dishwasher Sunday night, then Monday morning, we have all week to fill up those trash cans and try to stay on top of the housework.

You can see how getting these tasks done on the weekend will free your mind from the weight of fitting all these things in during the week.

SAVING YOUR LOVED ONE'S MEMORABILIA

In the survival phase, it is likely that you will lose—or have already lost—a loved one who was close to you. As you go through the grieving process, you also have to deal with the possessions they left behind. So how do you decide what to save when a loved one passes away?

My father passed away seven years ago. While there was a lot to do, I feel really blessed that my sister and I had a whole year to prepare for my father's passing. I think that if you wake up and somebody is just gone and there's no process to losing that person, it's much harder than when you have time to process and say goodbye.

It's also super hard when you have a loved one who is sick for longer than a year, or when they are in chronic pain, or when they are slowly losing their faculties due to dementia.

The last year with my grandfather was really hard for my grandmother. He died at 102, just a month shy of his 103rd birthday, but he was totally with it until he was 101½. But that last year and a half was really hard for her. He ended up having to go into an Alzheimer's unit for about eight months, which was very expensive and very hard. Eventually, he did not recognize her anymore.

I'm not going to go into all of the emotions and the different ways that people pass, but I just wanted to mention that I understand not everybody is in the same place when their loved one passes. Some are in shock, some have been expecting it for a long time, and some are just grateful that their loved one is no longer suffering. But no matter what the circumstances, those left behind face similar commitments and decisions. They must handle the estate, figure out what to do with their loved one's possessions, and work on processing their own feelings.

I've been working with a lot of people this last year who lost a spouse one year prior. They made it through the first year pretty well, but the second year is just so much harder.

The first year after they lose their loved one, I think many people say to themselves, "Okay, I can make it through this year. I can do this. This is the first time I have to do this alone. This is the first time I have to renew the car tags alone, the first time I have to do Christmas alone, the first time I have to go through my birthday alone."

Just like the little engine that could, they think, "I can do this, I can make it." And everyone around them is saying, "I know it's so hard this year, but we're with you." Then the second year they think, "Oh, I have to do

166   The Mindset of Organization

this the rest of my life without them. I don't have to get through just one year. I have to get through the rest of my life without them."

Also, I think some people think, "Great! Mom made it through the first year (or my sister made it through the first year). She's fine." I think it's a little bit more lonely the second year. It's a bit more real the second year.

I also suspect you get this internal monologue: "Well, I'm going to have to move on. I'm going to have to create new traditions. I'm going to have to create new hobbies, and I'm going to have to find new people to hang out with." I just think the grieving process is really hard. And in my observation, the whole process takes about five years.

Now with all that background, we're going to talk about the physical stuff that is left behind when a loved one passes. When my father passed away, my sister and I had the entire family home to deal with. The home was not packed to the brim, even though our family had lived there thirty-five years, because my mom had already taken her stuff out a few years prior. And my father was a neatnik. He would get rid of stuff regularly. With that said, there was still a tremendous amount of stuff in the house.

There's just no way around it when someone passes away. Unless they're already in a nursing home, there are going to be a lot of possessions that are left behind.

Once you've been through settling an estate, you look around your own house and you start thinking, "Holy cow! If I get hit by a bus tomorrow, somebody has got to take care of every single thing that is in this house."

Here's what happens. We're constantly bringing stuff into our houses, setting it down, saying we're going to get to it later. But when someone passes away, your family members come in and they find your pile of junk mail and think, "Mom touched this mail. We have to keep this mail." I know I'm kind of making light of it, but you know it's true.

All of a sudden, every single thing that person ever touched, ever thought about, or ever mentioned, is put on a pedestal. I remember walking into my father's house and thinking, "How do you choose?"

A couple of days before my father passed away, right before he slipped into a coma, I had gone into his bedroom and just looked around thinking, "Is there any more information I need from my dad? Any more decisions that I need him to make before I can handle the estate?"

I found his little jewelry box. It had maybe thirty or forty pieces of random things in there, even ball markers for golfing. Just random stuff.

We brought it into my dad, and we put a cutting board on his lap like a desk. We said, "Dad, tell us about this jewelry."

It was so cute. He had a hammer that he used like a gavel, and he told us all about the pieces of jewelry that were in the case. I wanted to know what was valuable, what was sentimental, what memories I could take with me into the future once my father passed.

I am so glad we did this, for two reasons. First, it was fun. Well, every minute with my dad was fun, but this was a special time to go through some memories together. And second, when he looked at the jewelry, he said, "Oh my gosh. Eighty percent of this is junk."

Now, I'm sharing this with you because when someone passes away (or there's a divorce), 50 percent of the time I'm going into a home as a professional organizer because that homeowner just needs help processing through the stuff. They need someone to say, "It's okay to let this go." And, "No, maybe you really should hold on to that even though you don't want to right now." We help you to not get rid of everything or not save everything. We can help pick out the salient things that are important to you.

There were things that I actually thought had value and had memories, and my dad said, "Yeah, this is trash," or, "This I got free and I never liked it. This is junk." And then he'd pull out something that I did not think was worth anything and say, "This is the most valuable thing in the box."

The women in my family live into their nineties, even to one hundred. I'm only in my forties now, but I fully plan on getting an A+ in life and making it to a hundred years old. However, I don't want my children to have to go through a whole jewelry box of stuff that I don't love. If I have jewelry that I don't love and I don't wear, and I don't want to give it to my daughter, I actually get rid of it on a regular basis. Because my thought is, whatever is in that jewelry box is stuff that I really, really love, that I want her to have, and that I want to be passed on to future generations.

One of the funniest things that we found in my childhood home when we were cleaning it out was a pencil from my elementary school, Bath Elementary. It's a little red pencil. I still have it and still write with it. Now that definitely is not something that needs to be saved. It's a thirty-seven-year-old pencil, but it was kind of fun to find that pencil from my childhood.

So I'm telling you, it doesn't matter what it is. You can save it. And it doesn't matter if it's a five-thousand dollar glass bowl, you can sell it. You don't have to keep it. There is nothing you have to keep, and there is nothing you have to get rid of.

How Families Make Choices

As I was working with my father's estate, I thought back to when I saw my father and his siblings divide his parent's possessions when I was thirteen. When dividing an estate, it can be helpful to have a model as an example to follow. Here is what I remember.

My father is the oldest of six children. So when his father passed away, all the children convened in the family house and divided the estate. I was only thirteen at the time, but I was the oldest of all of the grandchildren. It was my job during that week to take care of the cousins, entertain them, and, above all, keep them away from the adults.

I later learned that the siblings went in order of age and each picked an item. Then they would repeat the process, round-robin style. Of course, there were a few items that everyone wanted: their parents' wedding photo, the original forty-two-year-old letter from my great-grandfather to my grandfather, and my grandfather's purple hearts. All of these were treasured items to each family member.

So it was decided that all of these special items would be framed and distributed among the siblings, and then each Christmas, the siblings would hand their item down to the next sibling in the order and the youngest would pass his up to my father. Not only would this allow all of the siblings to share these special items, it would give them an additional reason to get together and see each other at Christmastime.

When my father passed, we still had some of the items my father took home that day, thirty years prior, that were not in the family rotation. Most notable were the Korean statues which Grandpa had gotten in the war. I said to my aunt, "These are yours, because they're your father's."

And I will never forget what my aunt said to me. "No, your father picked those things. They're yours. When we were picking money and jewelry, he was picking these specific memories that he had of his father. They are his now, so they are yours if you want them." In the end, for the most part, we did give them back to the siblings, because these items that my father had chosen to keep from his father didn't have the meaning for us that they did for our aunts and uncles.

I was very cognizant of the questions in my mind during that whole time we were going through my father's estate: "What do I really want? What does my sister really want? And what could the other family members possibly want?"

When you find yourself in this position, I want you to take some time for yourself. Go on a long walk, sit with a legal pad, drive for hours in your car where people can't get to you. And just think through every room in that house, the memories that you have with that person, and really ask yourself, "What does that say to me? Who is this person?" Make a list of one to twenty items that really represent that person to you.

My Grandfather: An Heirloom Memory

In January 2015, my grandfather passed away. He was 102. He lived a very full, very productive life. And I got to thinking about the items I have chosen to keep when a loved one passes away and how I made those decisions.

When my grandfather was in his late eighties, I actually had him make me a manger for our little china baby Jesus in our front hall. My grandfather was an engineer, and his gift to the world was being able to make beautiful things out of ordinary materials. Nobody else has this manger, and it wasn't something he had in his house that I got when he passed away. But when he made me it for me, I knew I was asking him to make me the thing that would remind me of him forever. When he passed away, I didn't need anything because I already had the memory of him in this manger.

And now that he has passed, I am so grateful that I purposely asked for this treasured heirloom to be created.

My Great-Grandmother: Buttons

When I was in college, my great-grandmother passed away. I have many fond memories of time spent with her in her retirement apartment. She was a very eclectic woman who collected businesses as well as items. She was a teacher, a floral store owner, and a restaurant owner. She was always doing something.

The time I spent with her was usually me coercing her into getting "organized." And boy, was that a challenge! Every drawer was a junk drawer, and my grandma didn't meet anything that she couldn't reuse or recycle. One of the things I used to love to do at her house was play with her buttons.

My mother had told me the story that, when I was a child, my great-grandmother would take a small button box with her whenever she wanted to go shopping. She would set me on the floor with my button box and I would play for an hour sorting buttons.

When my great-grandma passed away, I was allowed to have anything I wanted in her apartment. And I chose her buttons. The buttons remind me of my childhood, when I would sort the buttons, and of the days I would spend with my grandma sorting out her junk drawers.

It is a small memento that I can see every time I look at my bookshelf, and it has a very special meaning to me.

My Grandma: Functional Treasures

My grandmother turned ninety in March. I talk to her on the phone often, and I'm always trying to glean more information from her brilliant mind. She is analytical, hard-working, resourceful, and predictable. I love to talk to her about politics and finances because she has a perspective born of longevity that I cannot find from my peers. She is often able to temper my unbridled excitement about whatever is going on in the media by relating it to something that happened in the past, or to caution me about what she sees going on behind the scenes as she reads between the lines of the news coverage. The thing I love most about my grandmother is her mind.

As she has aged, she has started giving me heirlooms to keep. She has an amazing jewelry collection with an interesting story behind it. My grandfather loved to work on antique cars. And every time he would go buy something for one of his cars, she would take an equal amount of money and buy a piece of jewelry.

A few years ago, I was admiring an opal ring at Grandma's house. I love to hear the stories behind the jewelry purchases that she has made. This ring was bought when she and Grandfather were on the way back from their honeymoon in California. She never wore the ring.

She asked me if I'd like to have it. Of course I said yes! But I asked her if I could turn it into a necklace slide so that I would wear it more often. She said yes, and I wear it frequently.

More recently, Grandma gave me a little secretary desk the size of an end table. I remember seeing it at the end of her couches in all the different homes she lived in. This miniature desk has a door that folds down, which was just the right size to hold the pill-size metal painted boxes and small glass bowl of colorful marbles which she kept there.

I have always treasured this little desk. I love how it is miniature and yet functional, and it just reminds me of my grandma. This year, it came to reside in my bedroom office, and I use it daily.

How Do You Decide What to Keep From Your Parents?

Now when you think about your parents, you're likely going to get more than one thing. And you're allowed to have more than one thing. As a matter of fact, you can have it all. If you want to move right into their house, sell your house, and have all their possessions, that is your right. But I want you to think about what you'd pick if you could only have ten or twenty things. What would be the most important things to you? They do not have to make logical sense to other people.

I know quite a few friends, a lot of people actually, that keep the family home for a full year while they decide what to do with it and slowly sell the things from that estate.

My sister and I did not have the luxury of time. A few weeks after the funeral, I came up to the house and stayed for a week. I would get up early in the morning, go into whatever room we were going to go through that day, and pull everything that I could out of the drawers and the cabinets. I had already decided what I wanted in that room.

When my sister came over, we would start by picking an item we wanted and then giving the other person a turn. Back and forth until we were done. Since there were only two of us, it was pretty easy for us to each go through our lists of what we wanted in priority order. In the whole process, there were only a few items that we both wanted, and we easily came to agreements about those.

Don't let me fool you. It would have been easier if I was told I could only pick twenty things. After we chose what we wanted, we both took a whole bunch of additional items because we could. It was all ours. Paper plates, napkins, lightbulbs. I had a whole twenty-seven-foot U-Haul, so don't think that I only took ten things out of my family home!

The entire furnished area of my basement is pretty much a replica of my childhood home. You can walk into my basement and see the furniture, the pictures, the lamps, everything. It's all down there. It's been seven years. I really don't need most of that, but to be honest, it was nicer than what we had. So we got rid of what we had in order to have this nicer furniture in the basement. If we were moving tomorrow to a smaller place, some of it I would let go, some of it I would keep.

I had to make my decisions within a week and leave with the U-Haul. Then my sister had another month where she disseminated everything out to the family and handled the estate sale. I did not participate in that because I was too far away. Which is why I'm really grateful that, in Cincinnati, I'm able to do the same thing for other families. Like in my case, I had moved away from home over twenty years ago. I don't live in that area anymore. I don't even know where you would go to donate things there.

In Cincinnati, we fill that void. The parents have passed away, there's a house here, but all the children have moved away to New York, California, North Carolina, Florida, wherever they live now. They come in for the funeral and decide what they want, but they don't have the weeks that it takes to really clean out the house and prepare it for sale. So we do those services for them at Organize 365.

While I have not lost my spouse, I have helped many women who have. The process is very similar to the process my sister and I went through, with one huge exception. Spouses are living in the house with their spouse's possessions. The process of grieving and processing through a spouse's possessions takes a longer time and is usually done more gradually.

What About You?

You have a different relationship with everyone you know. The passing of a family member or friend is very difficult. Often, I see people fall into one of two camps. Either they want to keep every single possession that their loved one ever touched, or they default to saying, "No, that's okay, I don't need anything." And often the true answer is somewhere in the middle.

If you tend to say, "No, that's okay, I don't need anything," I encourage you to think of one thing that you would like from someone who has passed away. It can be as simple as a button box or as complicated as a handmade manger. And most likely, what you choose will not make sense to those around you . . . and that's okay. It's all about you.

If you tend to want to keep everything, go ahead. Fifty percent of the people I go in and professionally organize have lost a loved one in the last five years. The grieving process is long and individualized. The last thing you want to do is give up something you're not ready to give up yet.

As I've mentioned before, five years seems to be the magic amount of time that needs to pass before full closure seems to settle in. Having a professional organizer help you process through why you saved what you saved and how you could still remember your loved one without that physical possession, is an invaluable gift you can give yourself.

I encourage you to interview organizers before you hire them. Make sure that they are willing to spend the time to process through your emotions and not just help you declutter your house. The pace may be slower and the cost higher if you go this route, but you will feel satisfied and have more closure in the end.

Why Is This So Hard?

Why is it so hard to figure out what you want from an estate? Number one, I think it's hard because when you're in grief, you're just not thinking as clearly as you usually do. I really think it takes about five years to see any of what you've been through in a somewhat logical manner.

But I was thinking about how blessed I was when I went through the estate with my sister and how well we got along during that process of going through our father's house. It's not an easy thing to do, and we did a really good job getting along. I watch a lot of my friends who, with their children or their siblings, are going through their parent's house. It's stressful, it's hard.

People don't like change. And dealing with an estate, losing a spouse, or losing a parent is change. It means that forever forward, your holidays will be different. Forever forward, your everyday life will be different because this person is gone.

Not only do people not like change, but they really don't like change that they can't control. You didn't have control over when your loved one passed away. They just did. Sometimes you project that onto other things. You might say, "Well, I didn't have a choice on that, so I'm going to have a choice over this butter knife. We are going to have a to-the-death argument because I want this butter knife and you're not getting this butter knife because it's my butter knife." It's really not about a butter knife.

In my sister's case, she probably didn't have a choice about how quickly we settled the estate. Logically, she knew that I didn't have as much time as she did, and we didn't want to spend a lot of money keeping up a house that neither of us was going to live in. You may not have a say on the timetable. There may be something you really wanted out of that house and you didn't get. Even though you took a whole bunch of other stuff, the one thing you wanted, you didn't get.

It's so easy to know that you're not in control and be like, "Fine, I'm not in control of all these other things, but this one little thing, this is what I'm going to be in control of."

As you transition into the downsizing and legacy phase of life, the feeling of control ebbs and flows. One day you have it, and the next day you are floundering, struggling to understand the younger generations and their perspectives.

Phase Four

DOWNSIZING AND LEGACY

THE ROLE OF GENERATIONS IN ORGANIZATION

I am not in the downsizing and legacy phase of my life yet, but 50 percent of the Organize 365 clients are in this phase. We have helped hundreds of women as they downsize their homes and settle loved ones' estates.

As a professional organizer, one of the skills I have honed is that of being a generation translator. Last year, I read the book *Generations: The History of America's Future, 1584 to 2069* by William Strauss and Neil Howe. I have always been fascinated by history, large families, and group dynamics.

Generations was written in 1991 and analyzes the eighteen generations of Americans from the founding fathers through 2069. Strauss and Howe discovered, as I did, that there are four phases of life that a person goes through. They define these phases as Youth (birth to twenty-one), Rising Adulthood (twenty-two to forty-three), Middle Age (forty-four to sixty-five), and Elderhood (sixty-five and up).[4]

---

[4] Neil Howe and William Strauss, *Generations: The History of America's Future, 1584 to 2069* (New York: William Morrow & Company, 1991), 56.

What I found so interesting is that, while everyone goes through these phases, each generation does it differently. Strauss and Howe have defined four distinct generation types that cycle through on a predictable basis. The Pew Research Center generational time brackets and population sizes (in the US) as of 2014 are:

- The Silent Generation, born 1928–1945: 28 million.
- The Baby Boomer Generation, born 1946–1964: 74 million.
- Generation X, born 1965–1980: 64 million.
- The Millennial Generation, born 1981–1996: 68 million.
- Gen Z, born 1997–2015: No population figures listed.

Source: Pew Research 2015[5]

As Strauss and Neil describe the characteristics and traits of each generation, they alternate between recessive and dominant generations. For example, even though Generation X is in its prime influential years, almost all marketing is geared to the Baby Boomers and Millennials.

---

[5] Pew Research Center tabulations of the 2014 March Current Population Survey from the Integrated Public Use Microdata Series (IPUMS). http://www.pewsocialtrends.org/2015/03/19/comparing-millennials-to-other-generations/#!11.

Yes, I have a complex about this. I mean, come on. My generation is marked with an "X," for crying out loud. We didn't even get a real name. But I digress.

So what does this have to do with organizing your house? Actually, a lot. First, each generation views the world differently. As the Baby Boomers start to retire, they will not retire as their parents in the Silent Generation did. You can already see that Baby Boomers are retiring later and not as likely to move into retirement communities.

Another marked change is the way the current generations are moving into adulthood. Millennial children have lived at home much longer than the Baby Boomer and Generation X children did. They are changing jobs more often and delaying entrance into the home-buying market—or opting out of it entirely.

These differences in how each generation sees the world have a huge impact on how each generation organizes their homes and how many material possessions they keep. Most women in the Silent and Baby Boomer generations got married in their twenties, bought a house, and raised a family. They registered for formal china and had fancy parties in the seventies, eighties, and nineties. They bought a family home and may still live in that same home today. They save their memories through printed pictures, physical quilts, and lots of material possessions.

Downsizing for these generations is hard because the items they were told would hold their value, like china, baseball cards, and furniture, have not. The market is flooded with china patterns that the Millennial and Gen Z generations do not want.

Many Millennials and Gen Zers do not want physical photographs or quilts Great-Grandma made. Their generation is looking to make memories through new experiences, not hang onto the old ones through physical reminders.

So when a Baby Boomer mom is ready to gift her treasured heirlooms to her children and grandchildren, there is a disconnect. So many of my clients are frustrated that the items they have held on to for years are not worth much monetarily and may be worth even less as a gift.

Even when you look beyond the generational perspectives about "stuff," you can see that society as a whole is moving away from the accumulation of material possessions. Strauss and Howe address this trend in their book as well. Along with generational tendencies, there are moods. Strauss and Howe define the world view as vacillating from complexity to simplicity. According to them, we are at the beginning of a simplification cycle in history.

For those in the Baby Boomer and Silent generations, the act of downsizing tends to be more arduous than it is for Generation X and younger. Not only are they letting go of their physical possessions, but they often feel their memories and values are tied up in those items.

It is often an emotional and depressing undertaking because the legacy they thought they were creating is not as valuable or valued as they anticipated. Without understanding the generational filter, parents struggle to pass on their legacy to the next generation, and younger generations feel burdened by the physical weight of their parents' gifts.

Here are my suggestions for navigating these ever-changing trends.

#1 Come to terms with the fact that physical possessions do not hold the resale value they once did.

Our team does not prepare or hold garage sales, estate sales, or moving sales. The time investment is not worth the financial return. Yes, you can earn a few hundred to a few thousand dollars depending on what you have to sell, but in my experience, the tax benefit and the savings from donating your items is a better payoff.

#2 Make sure that someone wants what you are saving.

If your attic and basement are full of items for you to one day give to your children, do it as soon as possible. Why are you waiting? Spend the day together. Go down memory lane and fill their U-Haul. You will have greater pleasure seeing your treasures in use in their homes instead of crammed in your basement.

#3 Embrace the "less is more" philosophy.

You're downsizing, right? So do not be offended if your children do not want to upsize. Families are becoming more and more agile. People are moving more often, switching jobs, and having fewer children. Give your children fewer physical items and more experiences.

#4 Decide what memories you want to share with future generations, and be open to how you'll share them.

I love the feel of a physical scrapbook. I personally own a hundred, and I've made over three hundred for clients. My children are going to love the five I made for each of them, but not the ninety others. I know this. I still have all one hundred because I love them. And I still create physical scrapbooks for clients because I do not like digital photo albums. My clients enjoy the scrapbooks as soon as they are created.

However, I understand that many people in the Millennial and Gen Z generations will not want these albums. So I scan all of my clients' physical albums, save them to a backup hard drive, and upload them to Dropbox. I am also in the process of scanning all of my physical albums for my children to stream as a screensaver on their TVs.

Go ahead and create your legacy the way you want to enjoy it. Then partner with someone to translate that memory into a meaningful experience for future generations.

#5 Strive to understand change.

It is so hard to see future generations appear to disregard your contributions to society. We work so hard all our lives to better the generations that follow us. And by all appearances, it looks like no one cares. But they do.

Honestly, I am struggling to understand the Millennial sharing economy, the pace of technological change, and the on-demand availability of information. It has really helped me to understand the generational differences and to be able to filter information based on what age group I am talking to.

Change is change. It is not good or bad; it just is. Understanding that the next generations do not value physical possessions as much will help you to not feel devalued when your children do not want to have all of your stuff. And for the younger generations, understanding that your parents saved all this for you as a legacy and inheritance will help you understand their love for you and their care for your future.

So how do you decide what to keep and how many of each item you "should" have? It's time you learn the IDLE process.

THE IDLE PROCESS

In this book, I have purposely not created a room-by-room action plan for you to follow. I want to teach you how to look at an object and think like an organized person thinks.

How do we decide which objects to keep, where to keep them, how long to keep them—and what is the right number, anyway?

For example, we use box fans in our house. Every bedroom has a box fan. Around Christmas, we lost one, and I had to go buy a new box fan. But the box fan I bought was damaged. When I returned it to buy another box fan, I just went ahead and bought a second box fan to keep in my storage room in the basement.

Over the holidays many stores were closed, and it was really inconvenient not to have that fan in the hallway. So I decided to keep an extra fan on hand that I can go get any time a fan breaks. Then I can replace the storage room fan, as opposed to desperately trying to replace a fan we use every day.

So for us, having one extra fan in the storage room, plus the fans in use, is how many fans we need to have in our house. That's not something I've ever talked about on my blog or in my podcast. Clients look to me to tell them the magic number of items they need to keep for every single category of stuff in their homes.

How do you know how many fans to keep? Why would you or wouldn't you need an extra fan? How do you justify an extra fan if you decide to keep it? Here's the bottom line: there is not one right answer. I could have five fans in my storage room because I need that much security. And that would be okay if I consciously made that decision.

As a professional organizer, I guide my clients through a series of questions to find out what the perfect number of items is for them. Then we find creative ways to organize the items they want to keep.

Most of my clients think, "Oh my gosh, almost all the clutter that is left in my house right now is stuff that I don't feel like organizing. I don't want to make a decision about whether or not I want to keep it." Or, "I don't know how to store the things I want to keep in the space I have." Or my favorite, "I don't want to store it, but I can't get rid of it yet." So they delay the decisions and live with the clutter.

The reason why your garage gets so out of control is because you walk through the garage and you set things down. You tell yourself that you're going to come back and put it away, but you don't. Eventually you're just walking through piles of stuff in your garage because you never went back and put anything away. It was delayed decision-making.

Part of the reason that we are delaying the decision-making on some of the clutter in our homes is because we don't have enough information to decide if we want to keep that product or how many of that product we want to keep. It really comes down to your mindset.

Your mindset develops from the conditioned responses that you have to various things.

You have a mindset about everything. When you were reading my fan story, you likely had a monologue in your head. Some of you thought, "We don't need fans, why would you ever keep fans?" And others thought, "Oh my gosh, we would die if there wasn't a fan in every room. I think we need five in the storage room. That's a good idea. I never thought about putting five in the storage room. I'm going to go buy five fans today." That's okay. It doesn't matter which end of the pendulum you're on; just realize you do know what you want.

Learning to change your mindset about your clutter will help you make organizational decisions that you can then implement when you have the time to organize.

I realize most people don't have a ton of time to organize their house, and most people don't love to do it like I do. So when you do have the time set aside to organize your house, you would like to do it as quickly and efficiently as possible.

I was listening to a sermon one day, and the preacher said that you're never in idle. You're either moving forward or you're moving backward, but there's no such thing as idle. That message has always stuck with me.

Many professional organizers have acronyms for the process that they use to help you declutter and organize your home. As I was thinking about this, I came up with my own acronym: "IDLE." It stands for:

I	–	**Identify**
D	–	**Decide**
L	–	**Locate or Let Go**
E	–	**Evaluate**

Let me take you through this four-step process with one item. I've been organizing for fifteen years and phone books are something I have found in almost every single home that I have ever organized. And fifteen years ago, we definitely needed phone books. But in today's day and age, most people no longer need phone books.

It doesn't mean the phone company is not going to deliver them to you every single year, but most people no longer use phone books. I don't say everyone, because there are definitely people who do still use phone books. But I would say 80 percent of my clients now, when we come across phone books and I take them through the same conversation I'm about to take you through right now, decide they don't need phone books.

I - Identify: What Item Needs to Be Organized?

For this example, the item in question is phone books.

D - Decide: Yes or No?

Here's how this conversation goes.

We come across the phone books and I say, "Do you need to keep your phone books?" And 80 percent of the people say yes right away. "Yes, we need to keep our phone books." A few people say, "No, go ahead and recycle those." But when I leave the house, 80 percent of the people have recycled their phone books. So what happens to that 60 percent of people who say, "Yes, I need to keep the phone books" that makes them change to, "No, I can recycle the phone books" by the time I leave their houses?

Here's what happens. When we aren't sure if we need something, our default is to save it just in case. Always. Here's the key. If you're going to recycle your phone books, you have to know what you're going to do when you need to look up a phone number.

Do you realize that you can look up everything in the White Pages online for free? And for the most part, Google has replaced the Yellow Pages. Anything you would look up in the Yellow Pages, you can look up on Google.

If you're not on the computer very much, you may want to keep your phone book. If you advertise in the phone book and you want to compare your ads to other people's ads, you may want to keep the phone book. If you have a phone book from another city you frequent often, you might want to keep that phone book. So you have to decide: Do you want to keep the phone book or don't you want to keep the phone book?

What you're doing is changing your mindset about phone books. This is a technology that is becoming more outdated every year. Even if you decide to keep your phone books this year, you may decide three years from now that you no longer need to keep those phone books. So whenever a new phone book arrives on your driveway, you might want to have this conversation with yourself.

D - Decide: How Many?

Okay, so you've decided, "Yes, I'm going to keep my phone books" or, "No, I'm not going to keep my phone books." If you plan to keep them, the second decision you have to make is how many. How many phone books do you need?

Do you need the White Pages and the Yellow Pages and the phone books for the surrounding neighborhoods? Or do you just need the White Pages for the county that you live in? Do you want this year's and last year's or just the most current phone book?

Just make the decision. There is no wrong answer. Maybe you've decided, yes, you're going to keep them and you're just going to keep one set of White Pages and Yellow Pages combined. Or, no, you're not getting rid of any.

L - Locate or Let Go

The next step in IDLE is to locate or let go. If you've decided you're not going to keep phone books, you're going to let go and walk them straight out to the recycling bin and recycle them, and you're done.

If you decide that you are going to keep your phone books, then you need to decide where you're going to keep them. You're going to locate them somewhere in your house.

Many people keep them in a cabinet near the phone in the kitchen. Our family no longer has a home phone; everyone has cell phones. So our phone book doesn't have to be located in the kitchen. When we had phone books, I put ours in the front hall. It was easy enough to access them when we needed them, but it didn't take up prime real estate in the kitchen. So that's a good place to locate them.

E - Evaluate

The last step in IDLE is to evaluate. Every year or so, when you see a phone book, you're going to evaluate: Is this system still working for you? Do you still need to keep phone books?

Here is the best part. When you finish reading this chapter, you may or may not go find all your phone books. The whole point is that you've made a decision about your phone books. And the next time you run into phone books in your house, you will be able to instantly move them where you want them to be or declutter them because you've already made a decision about what you're going to do with your phone books.

Now, I realize making decisions about phone books is relatively simple. I used that example so you could see the whole decision-making process without the emotional overlay that usually clouds our decisions. Also, while it may be really easy for you to make a decision about phone books, I am sure you can think of a relative in your family who has years and years' worth of phone books and doesn't want to get rid of them.

Understanding the IDLE process will give you the tools to see why they are holding on to their phone books. Are they unsure of how to look up phone numbers online? Did they spend hard-earned money on Yellow Pages ads? Do they keep multiples so one is always within reach?

When I fail to put things away in my house, it's usually because I'm not sure I really want those things, but I don't know how to get rid of them. The more I'm able to make quicker, more informed decisions—to trust my gut and just do it—the happier I am, the less clutter I have, and the more I feel I have power over my stuff as opposed to being a slave to the things that I own.

It is so hard to be objective about items we really cherish and have collected over time. Very few of you had any heart palpitations as I discussed decluttering your collection of phone books. I have a feeling you don't feel that way about all the books in your house. Reading a book can transport you to another place or help you through a tough journey. They are a part of your story, but it might be time to let go of some of your physical books beyond just the phone books.

ARE YOUR MAGAZINES EMPTY COFFEE CUPS?

As a professional organizer, I am always trying to help my clients change how they think about their "stuff." Magazines are often a hot clutter item.

Usually, that's because we buy them or subscribe to them and "someday" we are going to read them.

I get that. Kinda. Once you pass fifteen subscriptions though, you lose me.

When I was younger, I used to like magazines. I never loved them. I think the reason why is because I want to complete things. When I start a jigsaw puzzle, I work like crazy to complete it in a couple of days. If I start a project, I want to finish it. I'm constantly checking things off my to-do list.

So even when I read a magazine, I am a horrible magazine reader. I'll get a magazine like *People* at the beach, and then I'll plow through it in an hour and a half like it's my job to finish it. Then when I get to the end of the magazine, I think, "Oh, I'm done." I didn't take the time to really enjoy it. I don't know. I'm just a horrible magazine reader.

Anyway, last week I was ready to launch into my magazine spiel with a client when she almost stumped me.

I was looking at stacks and stacks of magazines, which I assumed were yet to be read. My first question is always, "If you could only buy three magazines this week, what three would you pick?" As the color drained from her face, I quickly realized these magazines meant more to her than I had anticipated.

So I doubled back. "Which magazines do you sit down and read cover to cover as soon as you get them?"

She said, "I read them all cover to cover as soon as I buy them."

I was in shock. "All these magazines are read already?"

Yep.

I had to switch gears from finding time for her to enjoy what she had purchased, or limiting her future reading options, to seeing that she had already consumed the content that she had purchased.

And then it hit me.

When she told me that she'd read them all, I realized that she loves magazines. Like, she loooovvvvees magazines. She loves the experience of buying them. She loves the experience of reading them. And some of them, she will go back and read again.

I said, "Okay, well, this is awesome. This is great. I have never met anybody that would buy this many magazines and read them. Most people buy magazines and books as things they want to do, not things they're actually going to do today."

This was a new organizational problem. My next question was, "Why are you keeping them?" Well, she loved reading them. She really enjoyed it. So why would you get rid of something you love?

As luck would have it, I had actually been early to my appointment that day. I had stopped and bought a Starbucks coffee. I was a brand new coffee drinker at the time and I treated myself to a Tall Starbucks Caramel Macchiato. It was expensive, but I loved it. And so I bought it. I enjoyed it all the way to my client's house. And when I got there, I threw the cup away.

I said to my client, "You know, a Starbucks coffee is, like, three or four dollars, and I love it. I enjoy every single sip. And when I am done, I throw the coffee cup away. I don't keep the empty coffee cup to remind me how much I enjoyed drinking that Starbucks coffee."

She looked around the room and she said, "Oh my gosh."

I said, "Now how many of these magazines can we get rid of?"

She said, "Almost all of them."

I couldn't believe it. That analogy to her was enough for her to say, "You're right. I bought them. I enjoyed it. I drank it. I ate it. I'm done with it. I'm not going to read these fifteen magazine subscriptions again, but these four I am."

The other piece that really helped her let go of her magazines was the fact that her mother was in a retirement home. We realized she could be giving these magazines to the retirement home and then other people could be enjoying the magazines, too.

Now we also had a place for future magazines to go. Literally, thousands and thousands of magazines left that house that day because this woman's mindset shifted. Getting rid of items you love in your home does not discount the experience you had with that item.

I want you to think about all the magazines or books that you currently have. Can you find time in your week to read? I read books for hours on Sundays and sporadically during the week.

Do you have time on the weekend to enjoy a cup of coffee and read a magazine? Or do you have a time during the year when you can sit and flip through magazines? Maybe it's winter break, or maybe it's in July. Personally, I save any reading like that for our week at the beach. Once my pile starts to get too high, I eliminate a few.

Do you have a place you could put those magazines? And are there magazines that you're still paying for and getting that you don't read? If there are, cancel them. I'm giving you permission to cancel them.

The next time a child says, "Please sign up for this magazine for our school to make money," hand the kid ten bucks for their school and be done. Don't sign up for any more magazines.

Now let's talk about the magazines and books that are on your bookshelves, in your drawers, or that you have saved over the years. Many of my clients have scores of old magazines. Some of those magazines aren't even being published anymore. Some have great organizing ideas, decorating ideas, or recipes.

I want you to really think about where you get your decorating, organizing, and cooking ideas from these days. For most people, it's Pinterest.

We organized a house a few years ago that was a corporate relocation. The client had every single room painted before she moved in. The colors in this house were amazing. A rich purple, a lot of trendy gray, and a cool slate blue. I asked her, "Where did you find these colors?" And she said, she went to Houzz. She gave the colors to the painter and they were perfect.

If you're keeping old decorating magazines, old cooking magazines, or old organizational magazines, are you going to go there when you actually need ideas? Those older architectural magazines are beautiful, but they're very dated. So you wouldn't really use those ideas. You could with cooking magazines, but trends in cooking change as well, so if you want the latest trend in cooking, you're going to do the new things that are out there now.

So really think about the different magazines that you have and ask yourself: Are you going to go back to those magazines again?

You might be reading this and thinking, "Oh, she's right. I don't need those magazines at all," but inside you're thinking, "I'm not getting rid of them. I don't care what she says. That woman is crazy. Why am I getting rid of all those? Do you know how much money I paid for those? They are all organized. They're on the bookshelf. They look nice."

That is the first step. This is all about your mindset, thinking about magazines differently. Not necessarily going and gutting your magazine bookshelf, but thinking, "Okay, am I going to read the next magazine that comes into the house? When am I going to read it? Am I paying for it? Do I want to pay for it?"

When you look at your bookshelf, think, "Okay, I read those. I loved that. That was my hobby then. Is it my hobby now? Do I really want to read that again? Or am I kind of over it?"

What I find with most of my clients is that the majority of people can get rid of 30 percent at a time. So let's say you have three different magazine collections. You may say, "She's right. I'm never going to do those decorating ideas from the eighties. I'm going to get rid of that set of magazines, but I'm going to keep these other two sets because I still like them."

Six months or a year from now, you are going to look at those magazines again, and you're going to hear these words in your mind about making decisions about magazines. You might think, "You know what, I have two sets of magazines here, but this one I really don't love anymore. I'm just going to keep this one set of magazines." Then the third time through, you might get rid of that third set. Or you might never get rid of it.

Another client we were working with had a bazillion, million, trillion magazines. I'm not even kidding you. And she did not want to get rid of any of them. None of them. Not at all.

We organized all of the magazines in one area by title. Once they were sorted, she could see that she had thirty different magazine subscription sets, some of which went all the way back to the eighties. When she could see everything she owned at one time, in one location, she was able to say, "Half of this can go."

When everything isn't in one location, and you visually can't see and process it all at once, it's hard to get rid of things because you don't know how much you have. It is also much harder to make decisions one magazine at a time instead of by piles of magazine titles.

If you have one hundred magazines that cover ten subscriptions, it is much easier to sort your magazines into ten stacks and decide all at once what you want to do with each stack than to decide one magazine at a time.

I encourage you to save whatever you want to save, but locate it in one place. Your magazines go here on a basement bookshelf. Take all of the magazines that you've decided to save, and put them in one location. Just the act of putting them in one location will make you think even deeper about how many you want to save, when you're going to enjoy them again, and what you're saving them for.

Now that you understand the phases of life and have some ideas for preserving memories and processing your stuff, let's get down to the brass tacks about how to start organizing your whole house.

SKILLS

~~~

WHERE DO YOU START?

Maybe you're overwhelmed and you just don't even know where to start on a task this big. Or, more likely, you just don't have enough time to get the job done. You maybe know where to start. But even if you started there, there's no way you would finish, so what's the point of starting, right?

The answer is, just start. I know, it's so cliché. "Oh, just start. If only she could see the mess that I have." Trust me, I've seen the mess that you have. I know what you're looking at, but it is just about starting.

If you were going to start a diet, you would just have to start. Eventually, you just have to start. It's going to take time. It is probably going to take at least a year, but that's okay. You're going to make progress.

#1 Take pictures.

The first thing I want you to do is to go around your house and take pictures of everything: every closet, every room, every drawer. I want you to take hundreds of photos of every single area and upload them to Dropbox, because here is what's going to happen. You're going to start, I know you are, and all you are going to see is what you have left to do. You are not going to see what you have already finished. Every time you walk in the house, the thing that is not done is the thing that is going to drive you crazy, as opposed to the eighty things that you already have done, that are functioning and working well.

#2 Get your Sunday Basket working.

Before you tackle organizing the whole house, get your Sunday Basket working. Knowing where all your actionable papers are and having a place to drop notes to yourself is the foundation of an organized home. Get your foundation in place first.

#3 Prepare.

Before you get started, I want you to prepare. I suggest getting two colors of trash bags. I have white for trash, which is a smaller, regular kitchen trash bag, and then I get the black trash bags for donations. I buy my bags from Costco.

#4 Purge.

The first thing I want you to do in your space is purge. I want you to declutter, and I want you to get rid of things. We cannot organize clutter. We tend to hold on to things longer than we need.

Pretend that you're going to move to Europe, and you're only allowed to take three suitcases. Ask yourself, "Am I really going to wear this again? Do I really like it? How do I look in it? Am I really going to lose that weight? Could somebody else use this?" and ultimately, "Would I rather have my space organized? Know what I have in there? Know I can grab anything out, put it on, and go to work and feel great? Or would I rather have this thing just in case for someday?"

We tend to not want to get rid of stuff because we might need it one day, but in doing that, we're giving up the freedom-filled life of having an organized space.

So remember that. Every time you're holding on to something just in case, you're holding on to something that is keeping you away from that organized feeling that you want. Here are the questions I want you to ask yourself when you're holding these items.

Do you love it? If you say, "Oh my gosh, I love this. Like if I lose ten pounds, I am definitely going to wear this thing again," then keep it. But if you say, "Well, if I lose ten pounds, I think I looked okay in it," then no, we don't need to keep it.

Do you need it? If you say, "I don't like how much space this takes up, but we really do use it every year and I need it," well, you need to keep it, even though you don't love it.

If you don't remember what it is, you don't need it. I love when I'm with clients or by myself and I find things and think, "Now, what is this for?" If you don't know what it's for, you don't need it. Even if it's a piece or a part, you don't need it. The guy who comes to your house to fix whatever it is has all of those pieces in his truck.

Now if you (or your spouse or your dad or somebody else) are really mechanically inclined, then definitely keep it, label it, and know where it is. But if that is not you, you don't have to keep it. And you don't need to keep all the manuals that go to everything because you're not going to fix those things. You can go ahead and get rid of them. They are all available online anyway.

Donate liberally. Take the bags straight to your car. Even if you're not going to go to Goodwill for a week, I don't care. Put them in the car because if they're in the car, they're more likely going to get donated than if you put them in the garage or leave them in your bedroom.

At the end of the day, it's going to be awesome. You are going to feel like your house has lost a ton of weight. And a lot of clutter is going to be gone. I want you to really enjoy what you have just decluttered. Even if it is just the drawers in your kitchen and you've donated three small boxes of things to Goodwill, you've made huge progress. At the end of each day, take pictures of what you have done and the progress that you've made.

I know you are thinking, "I'm not going to see a really big difference in the before-and-after pictures," which is what I often think, but I'm always wrong.

If you need to, make those "after" pictures a screen saver on your computer or your phone, or print them and put them up on a bulletin board or the refrigerator. Keep track of the progress you're making, because you *are* making progress, and you can do this.

#5 Once you clear the clutter, pick a comprehensive home organization plan.

A. The Room-By-Room Organization Plan

I suggest starting in the rooms you have the most control over so that the organization does not get undone as soon as you leave the room!

When my kids were little and my hubby and I spent the day cleaning, I would always tell him to leave the family room for last because the kids were playing in there. At the end of the day, he'd say, "You're right! There is no point in cleaning the room they are in!"

Step 1 – Pick a room you control.

Start with your closet, the laundry room, the home office, or the kitchen. Then move on to the family room, kids' rooms, garage, and pantry.

Once you pick your space, stop and think about what is working and what is not working. And not everything is "not working."

There are some things that are working. What are they? Why do those work for you? Can you apply that thought to the areas that are not working?

Step 2 – Decide how much time you have to devote to this project today.

If you have the whole day, empty out the space, purge, and then put back what you want to keep.

If you have a limited amount of time, divide your space into three or four sections and work one section at a time. Empty the space, purge, and put back what you want to keep.

Step 3 – DO IT!

No, it's not going to be perfect.

Yes, you are going to get overwhelmed.

No, you won't have the "perfect" organizers to put your stuff in when you're done. You can shop for the organizers after you know what you're going to keep.

In my experience, it takes organizing a space about three go-rounds to really get it picture perfect.

The first time, you are overwhelmed and purge items that are older than your children.

The next time, you do a deeper pruning and get rid of some older "favorites" that you can live without.

The third time, if you haven't used it in six months, you pitch it. You enjoy knowing what you have and where it is way more than simply having stuff.

I know this was true for me with my master closet.

I just organized my closet again recently. It took me two hours. I got rid of two garbage bags of clothes and it felt great.

You'll get there, too!

B. The Whole House Method

Some of my clients either could not afford the room-by-room method or were so overwhelmed that it would have been pointless to completely deep organize their kitchen when the rest of their house was causing them so much stress!

So I started offering a whole-house purging session. These sessions are exhausting and a great workout. I have the clients schedule AMVETS to come to the house the next day because we often fill the garage with donations and trash.

This is not a day when we reminisce about a picture we find or plan how to create new systems. Oh, no. It's a fast-paced "save the house" mission.

Step 1 – Decide how much time you have to devote to this project.

This can be done in short spurts daily (like twenty minutes), but I prefer to set aside a big chunk of time, something like six hours or, better yet, the whole day. It is so worth it!

Step 2 — *Make a list of ALL the areas that are cluttered and stressing you out.*

List every room. I suggest leaving the garage, basement, and outside areas off your list.

Then divide the amount of time you have by the number of areas you need to tackle.

Often my clients will list:

- Kitchen
- Master bedroom
- Kids' rooms
- Family room
- Office

Notice that we're not looking at closets either.

About one to one-and-a-half hours per room will suffice.

Step 3 — *Prepare!*

You will need to know where you'll be putting trash and donations. I suggest the garage, if at all possible. Most of my clients will agree to park outside until trash day.

If your garage is full, that is okay. Just find another location where you can put the bags.

Buy the more expensive black flex trash bags. You will thank me. Have a different color of trash bag for actual trash. As the day goes on, the different colors will help you remember which bags are trash and which are donations.

Find a place for the kids to go that day and have some quick meals ready for your break time. You will work up an appetite.

Step 4 – *PURGE!*

Start in the first room, the kitchen. Set the timer for whatever amount of time you have for that space.

Your goal is to pitch anything that is trash first. If you get stuck on something, put it down and move on. Keep up your momentum.

Next, if you don't:

- Love it
- Need it
- Or remember what it is

Donate it!

If you aren't done before the timer goes off, move on to the next space anyway. If you have time, you can come back.

At the end of the day, most of the clutter should be gone, and what is left now needs to be organized.

But you still have closets, drawers, etc. to go through in each space. Once this "mass purging" has taken place, you can then go back and use the room-by-room method of organizing to really hone in on systems that will work for you and your family.

Maintenance

Once your home is organized, everything seems calmer and easier.

I bet that's what it's like if you lose a lot of weight. You are still in awe that you did it and nervous you will gain it back.

My husband and I are both working harder at putting things away and taking time to pick up the last five to ten items that are left out.

In the past, I would just wait until there was more to clean up. Now, I put those few items away so the room is completely clutter free.

It is SO nice to come downstairs to a perfectly clean kitchen and family room. It is equally nice to walk into a straightened and clutter-free bedroom at night. BUT it does take work, discipline, and focus.

I have been working a lot this week, and last night I noticed:

- my bathroom counter was getting piles
- I had three days of unopened mail in my Sunday Basket
- my car was still full from the last organizational job I finished

- there were a ton of leftovers in the refrigerator

SO . . . we had leftovers for dinner. I cleaned the bathroom counter while my bath was running. My mail can wait until Sunday. And I will get my car cleaned out tomorrow morning.

I live my life to overflowing, so my home will never be perfect. But I am striving to put more emphasis on maintenance so that I can spend my time helping others live a less cluttered life, too!

Maintenance is the key to staying organized. If you have kids, you may have noticed that when they're small, it's best to spend a few minutes at the end of the day picking up the kiddos' toys and getting ready for tomorrow. If you don't, the toys will take over the house in no time.

Years ago, as I started getting our house back on track, I noticed that not only had I taken on the job of organizing the whole house—I had to maintain the areas I had already purged and organized.

Around day twenty of doing the whole-house organization challenge the first time, I started doing the Zamboni Sweep.

Have you ever watched a Zamboni clean the ice during the Olympics? I became the Zamboni.

I started in the family room and kept walking around, picking up items and depositing them in their proper homes. I felt like a Zamboni because I did not let myself stop walking! In and out, around and around, but no stopping.

Crazy as it sounds, I am able to pick up and straighten quickly with my Zamboni method.

<u>If you need to stop and sit, you are organizing, not maintaining</u>. So any area that continually got cluttered, I would reevaluate and change so that I could just "Zamboni" it the next time.

NEXT STEPS

Where are you in your journey? What phase of life are you in?

Organization is a skill to be learned and developed over time. Your organizational mindset is being transformed. As you travel through each phase of life, how you use your space will change. You'll need new organizational systems. It's a process. You will never fully "get organized," but you can live a more organized life every day.

The hardest part about getting organized is completing each phases' cycle by taking care of the mementos you stored from that time of your life. Each cycle starts with accumulating what is needed for that phase and ends with saving the best from those years.

Organization involves constant pruning. The key is learning to let go of physical objects while retaining the memories associated with them. We are so blessed to be able to receive and give possessions freely. The more we give away, the more memories can be made.

In the afterword, I've included two whole-home organization options for you. I'm here to cheer you on as you take back control of your home and start to live a more organized life.

Afterword

THE WHOLE HOUSE CHALLENGE OPTIONS

OPTION #1 THE 40 WEEKS 1 WHOLE HOUSE CHALLENGE

The 40 Weeks 1 Whole House Challenge is the annual free program I offer at www.Organize365.com.

This is the original challenge I made for myself in January 2012. It is structured to match the forty weeks of the school year, running from the Monday before Labor Day through Memorial Day.

Each week, there is a blog post with a podcast to guide you through taking the next step to reclaiming your home. You can also download the Organize 365 app to follow along.

While the 40 Weeks 1 Whole House Challenge is a great place to start, it does have some limitations. That challenge was based on my house in the Midwest USA, when I had two preteen kids. I wasn't thinking about downsizing or the different configurations of homes around the world. The plan is also not as detailed as some people would like.

OPTION #2 THE 100 DAY HOME ORGANIZATION CHALLENGE

The 100 Day Home Organization Challenge is a faster and more detailed home organization program, designed to get your home organized in the most logical order without the organization being undone as you move to the next space.

This is a collection of a hundred daily actionable steps, along with videos and links to supporting podcasts and blog posts. The goal: to get your whole home organized in a hundred days.

The 100 Day Home Organization Challenge covers the main areas every homeowner needs to deal with:

- Kitchen and Food Organization
- Master Bedroom, Bath, and Closet Organization
- Home Office, Books, and Electronic Organization
- Garage and Storage Room Organization
- Laundry Room and Cleaning Supply Organization
- Family Living Space Organization
- Home Maintenance Binder and Light Paper Organization

According to a Boston Marketing Firm, the average American wastes fifty-five minutes a day looking for things they own but can't find.[6] So we are spending the time either way.

And while I designed the challenge to be completed in as little as fifteen minutes a day . . . Let's be honest. The real reason people want a fifteen-minute-a-day challenge is because they are overwhelmed, exhausted, and scared.

- Overwhelmed at the disorganized state of their home
- Overwhelmed at the energy it will take to do it all
- Overwhelmed at the idea of learning a different way of doing things
- Exhausted from daily life
- Exhausted from looking for things and frustrated that they can't find them
- Exhausted from living this way
- Scared it works for everyone else, but it won't work for them
- Scared they will pay for the course, but not take the action

[6] *Newsweek* (June 7, 2004)

- Scared to face the fact that this must change and, by committing to this challenge, they have to change

What I have found is that the time limits fade once you see results.

Time and time again, our clients keep organizing when we leave their homes at night. And once you decide it's time to get organized, you are going to be staying up late and gleefully organizing on the weekends, too.

I know it sounds crazy, but it's true. You will.

Because it's not about the amount of time you have.

Once you see that this works and you can do it, you'll be empowered. You will start to look forward to making the decisions about where you stuff goes instead of living in the exhaustion and stress of your stuff telling you how to feel.

It's not all rosy.

As you can tell, I am an optimist. I'm one of those "always happy even on rainy days" kind of people.

But this is hard, and it does take time to dig out of the chaos. And while this is a hundred-day challenge, I myself needed to do the challenge three times before my home felt really organized. That's true for most of my clients as well.

Once you buy this membership, you can do the challenge as many times as you want. Your membership will never expire.

The first three to four weeks will be rough. Your inner voice will make up reasons why you don't have the time, energy, or skills to do this, but you do!

And the mess will talk back to you, too. You will feel like you should be making more progress, faster.

But then it will happen.

After Day 22, you will walk into your kitchen and it will be organized!

And on Day 40, your master bedroom, bath, closet, and accessories will all be completed as well.

This will give you the power to move on to your books and office area.

So, if you are READY for a change, here is what the One Hundred Day Home Organization Challenge includes:

- One hundred days of daily organization tasks
- Weekly printable checklists
- One hundred daily videos
- Links to related podcasts and posts
- A private Facebook Community where Lisa comments daily

Sign up for your free trial week here: http://organize365.com/book-bonus/
I can't wait to help you get organized!

ABOUT THE AUTHOR

s a professional organizer and productivity expert, Lisa Woodruff has helped thousands of women reclaim their homes and finally get organized with her practical tips, encouragement, and humor through her blog and podcast at Organize365.com.

She is the creator of the online organization series which includes "The 40 Weeks 1 Whole House Challenge," "100 Day Home Organization Challenge," "Organize 101: The Sunday Basket," and "Get ALL Your Papers Organized."

Lisa has been featured in the *Huffington Post*, *Ladies Home Journal*, *Woman's Day*, *US News & World Report*, and *Getting Organized* magazine. She has appeared on Fox News 45 Dayton, Fox 19 Cincinnati, WKRC Cincinnati, *Living Dayton*, and numerous podcasts.

Lisa lives in Cincinnati with her husband Greg and two teenage children Joey and Abby.

41709113R00130

Made in the USA
San Bernardino, CA
18 November 2016